RENEGADE
AGENCY

Designed by Damonza.

ISBN: 979-8-9914664-0-0

RENEGADE AGENCY

A MEMOIR OF A FAMILY IN
CRISIS AND THE SYSTEMS
MEANT TO PROTECT US

ANDREA VERBANIC

Author's Note

All names used are pseudonyms except for myself and my family members. I want to bring attention to the systems that sometimes fail us more than the individuals involved in my case.

I was afforded the opportunity to listen to audio recordings and review investigative reports. I was initially hyper-focused on taking dialogue verbatim from the recordings but agreed to occasionally alter formatting for readability. Dialogue included in this book is an accurate representation of what was said on audio recordings with no distortion of intent or sentiment.

I have changed certain details of anecdotes about my former clients to protect confidentiality.

Prior to publication, I sent emails to key individuals extending an opportunity for them to provide context behind their decisions or simply give a statement that I would include in an epilogue. I conveyed that I would be fair, that I did not intend to humiliate them, and that I would not distort their words. I did not receive replies.

This book is dedicated to the children and families who receive services from state agencies and may find their lives irrevocably altered as a result. Your struggles buoyed my faith in my story, and I hope you find some measure of solidarity and comfort in what I've written.

PART ONE

Chapter 1

The First Interview

I DID NOT expect to be sitting in a police station lying through my teeth, but that's exactly where I was. The interview had been easier than I thought it would be, until right at the end when Kansas Bureau of Investigation agent Daniel Holland said, "Will you take a polygraph?" This surprised me because polygraphs had never been used in any of the cases I worked. I hadn't prepared for it to be a possibility.

Buying time so I could think, I asked, "Is anybody else taking one?"

"I can't tell you that."

Of course he couldn't. I quickly considered my options. Declining to take one would make me look guilty, but failing a polygraph—a very distinct possibility considering that I was lying—could also help land me in jail. What choice did I have? It filled me with anxiety, but I told Holland, "Sure, I'll take one."

Surprisingly, I hadn't been all that nervous during the interview until Holland asked me to take the polygraph. Lying wasn't hard because I was only omitting one thing, and everything else happened just like I said it did. I didn't have to keep track of anything I had made up because I hadn't made anything up. I only failed to mention something, which is the same thing as lying only easier.

⁊

December 2, 2013, was a Monday. On Wednesday, December 4, 2013, my twin boys and I were at Union Station in Kansas City, Missouri, riding the Christmas train and checking out the model train exhibit, when my phone rang. When I answered, the voice on the line said, "This is special agent Daniel Holland from the Kansas Bureau of Investigation." I thought, *The KBI? Where is this coming from?* By this point, I knew I was being investigated by the police, but I was expecting the assigned officer to be from Topeka or Kansas City. The KBI's entry into the investigation added anxiety to a situation that was already fraught with tension. It scared me, but I didn't waver. I had decided to lie in the very beginning and for now, at least, I was sticking with it. I steadied my voice on the phone and told Holland I was glad he called to schedule an interview, which was true. I wanted to get it over with.

December 5, 2013—the day of the first of three interviews— was the third working day after Abigail's injury was discovered. Going into the interview, I didn't know what work had been done on the case prior to my interview, who had been interviewed, when they had been interviewed or by whom, or what anybody had said. The purpose of a suspect's first interview is to obtain the initial version of events, so I expected to narrate my day from start to finish.

I'm one of those annoyingly chipper morning people, so on December 2, I was up at 5:30 a.m., walked the dog, went to the gym, meditated, and showered. I woke my two-year-old twins, Thomas and Joseph, around 7:30 a.m. so we could drive my older son, Ryan, to school, and I was back to greet fourteen-month-old Abigail Holder when she was scheduled to arrive at 8:00 a.m.

In my interview, I started when Abigail entered my house with her dad, Steve. "I could tell she was a little tired," I told Holland. "Steve said she had 'a case of the Mondays.' He said she woke up at 5:30 that morning. She was used to the routine and hadn't cried at drop off in a while, but on this day she did." I blamed Abigail's mood on the holiday break and told Holland that she most likely cried because I hadn't seen her for four days and she was out of routine.

Half an hour later, at 8:30 a.m., I settled all the kids down for breakfast, but Abigail didn't want to eat. "She just sat there," I told Holland "She didn't eat her toast." I didn't leave out a single detail in my account of our early morning. I included every bathroom break, diaper change, and nap.

Unstructured time with three toddlers can easily devolve into chaos, so each day I did my best to channel my inner preschool teacher. I always came prepared with two or three morning activity options, and this day I had yoga, finger painting, and music time on the docket. My kids were old enough to get into the yoga poses on their own, but I had to position Abigail in down dog because she couldn't do it herself. Babies doing yoga is hilarious, so I made sure to take a picture and send it to Abigail's mother, Meredith. Thomas and Joseph made a huge mess finger painting, but Abigail was reticent. I took her little hand and rubbed it in the paint, but she never did it herself.

I told Holland, "I took Abigail's shirt off so that her clothes wouldn't get messy, but she didn't finger paint. She just sat there, but she's not always very animated at my house." Abigail's mood changed for the better when I brought the music tub out. This was no surprise because she loved the music tub. All the kids did. It was filled with all the noisy things kids like: cymbals, maracas, sandpaper instruments, and bongo drums. Abigail chose the sanders and maracas and also took a turn on the drums. She looked so cute banging on the drums that I sent a video of it to Meredith.

Each day around midmorning, we would take a little field trip to make things more interesting for the kids and for myself. That day I packed the kids into the van and drove to Lawrence, Kansas, to look at Christmas trees that had been decorated to raise money for a children's shelter. Abigail fell asleep on the way. I didn't usually let the kids sleep much during the day, so they wouldn't be up late at night. Today though, I let it slide. Steve had said Abigail woke up early, so I figured she needed the extra rest.

I was adept at taking the children on outings, but I admitted to Holland that I was a little tense at the Festival of Trees. Normally our outings consisted of walking in the woods or going to parks, where there's little danger of ruining anything. The Christmas trees were a different story, though, because people did a lights-out job of decorating them. I wanted to see them, and I knew I could handle the potential chaos. I never took the kids anywhere that might be out of my comfort zone.

Abigail was always extremely well-behaved and did as she was told, but my kids could sometimes be little wild men. When Holland asked for more on that, I explained, "My twins sometimes run in opposite directions, and it's a nightmare." I told Holland that Joseph ran down a hallway leading off the stage where the trees were, and I had to run after him to bring him back. I explained that as we were walking through the Festival of Trees, Abigail would occasionally fall a step behind and her wrist would twist in my hand as she stumbled before I caught her. She didn't cry about this, though. I told Holland for the first of what would be many times, "There were no injuries and nothing was out of the ordinary." I didn't worry at all when describing our outing to him.

The kids and I meandered down the street after we finished walking through the Festival of Trees to window shop. Thomas and Joseph had tucked a few small digging toys in their pockets and pulled them out to play in the dirt under a tree for a bit.

Abigail sat on the sidewalk and watched but didn't participate. This wasn't unusual. She was an avid people-watcher, so she was in her element. The sweetest picture I took that day was of Abigail smiling on the sidewalk. Even after everything that happened later, my heart is still happy when I look at it. Abigail is in a pink winter coat zipped all the way to her neck with the hood pulled up. Sprouts of hair are lying on her forehead, her little cheeks are chubby, her eyes are clear and blue, and she has a sly smile on her face that announces to the world, *I'm adorable and adored.* I sent that picture along with another one of all three kids by a Christmas tree to Meredith.

As long as the kids were having a good time, I didn't have a problem staying out a little later. The digging took more time than I anticipated, and we found ourselves driving home later than we should have, with Abigail crying the entire way home.

"This was the most upset she got that day," I told Holland. "This wasn't abnormal." Abigail was only fourteen months old, so running close to lunch and nap time affected her more than it did Thomas and Joseph, who were a year older. I told Holland, "It wasn't abnormal for her to want to sleep on the way back home. I didn't let her sleep, so she cried for the entire drive. She had done this before, though." The words *normal* and *abnormal* are ones that I use repeatedly to describe Abigail's behavior that day. *Nothing was abnormal. Everything seemed normal.* Sometimes I'd substitute *Nothing was out of the ordinary* or *Nothing was unusual,* but the sentiment is the same. Nothing that happened during our day was different from what had happened on many days before.

I continued, "When we got home, she was still screaming. I got the kids out of the car and she was still screaming. But this was not abnormal for Abigail." At home, the boys immediately gravitated to our sandpile while I tended to her. I thought through the best options for getting her inside. If I carried her inside but left the bags and coats in the van, then I would have to leave her inside and go back out to get them. She wasn't coping well and I didn't want to leave her alone, so I decided to carry everything in together. Up the stairs I went with three children's coats, a purse, a diaper bag, and a screaming baby. Though impractical, this choice was standard for me.

We live in a bilevel, so I walked in through the garage and up the first set of stairs. This part of the journey went okay, but Abigail started to slip in my arms at the landing. I made it up the stairs and tried to go through the gate, but I got stuck because of everything I was carrying. As I tried to push my way through, Abigail continued to slip, and she was not happy about it. I tried to go through again but I wasn't successful the second time either. I told Holland, "She was still screaming, so I pushed my way through the gate and ended up knocking one side of the gate loose."

I thought I had handled myself well in the interview because I was simply narrating events exactly as they had happened. The next step in my day is what I had previously decided to omit from my interview. There was no dramatic soap opera pause here. I wasn't experiencing inner turmoil while thinking, *Here's my chance to be an honest person. Should I take it?* Instead I thought, *Here's the part where you lie. Just skip over it and go on to the next thing.* Fortunately, Holland made lying easy. He hadn't asked me any hard questions to this point and he hadn't challenged me on anything. He had spent the majority of the interview quietly listening.

Per my plan, I moved straight from the gate incident, skipped over what I had chosen to omit, and jumped straight to an explanation of retrieving the boys from the sandpile for lunch. The twins ate, but Abigail barely touched her food. I was surprised by this because she loved veggie burgers and she also hadn't eaten breakfast. I thought she must be feeling terrible because of her teeth. She picked at her burger a little bit, but not enough to count. I told Holland that during lunch "she just sat there."

Abigail fell asleep in her highchair, and I took this as a sign that she was done for the day. I skipped pre-nap stories and wrapped her up in her blanket. She slept soundly for two hours. During my break, I ordered a few Christmas presents and did a little hand sewing on the Christmas stocking I was making for Thomas.

Meredith was a little late to pick Abigail up. I told her that Abigail didn't eat that day and appeared to have a "holiday hangover," as we were coming off the Thanksgiving weekend. She said that Abigail was probably just cranky because she was teething and added that she woke up moaning three times in the night. I didn't tell Holland what Meredith said. I started to, but thought better of it because I thought it might make it look like I was pointing fingers. I described how Abigail whined and cried when Meredith put her coat on.

Holland asked, "Did you notice any changes in her behavior?"

"No, it was a pretty normal day." This was the truth. There wasn't even a change in demeanor after the event I lied about. She had been crying for quite a while before it happened—all the way from Lawrence, in fact—and she continued crying afterwards.

Holland asked, "Did you notice her favor her arm?"

I replied, "She didn't eat like normal. I remember her picking stuff up, but she didn't eat like normal." There's that word again: *normal*. Not wanting to eat is *normal* when you're teething.

I remember thinking how easy the interview had been to this point. More importantly, I remember believing that I was going to get away with it. If all Holland was going to do was sit quietly and barely ask me any questions, then this whole thing would soon be just a stressful blip in my timeline. But when he asked me to take a polygraph at the very end of the interview, I snapped back to reality. This was going to be way more complicated than I had let myself believe.

I was unaware of it at the time, but there were a multitude of questions Daniel Holland could have asked me during this interview. He could have challenged me on many elements of my statement, because some of the information I gave didn't match what Steve and Meredith had already told him. The accounts of Abigail's behavior contained some glaring inconsistencies and points of interest that Holland could have taken advantage of. He didn't, though, and he could have saved me six years of stress and heartache if he had.

⁂

This is a story of how I investigated child abuse reports for the State of Kansas for ten years and later found myself accused of child abuse by the same agency I used to work for. Shame frequently prevents those who have been investigated by the child welfare system from coming forward to describe their version of events. Consequently, society views the police, social workers, and doctors who investigate the reports as heroes and the suspects as villains without realizing that reality can sometimes be very different. My story matters—not just to me, but to others who might find themselves in a similar position. I'm providing my perspective and pray that my experience will help level the playing field.

The story I'm about to tell sounds so crazy you might be inclined to think I made it up, but I didn't. It's all true. Nothing about the routine events of December 2, 2013, gave me any indication it was going to be a day that would eventually compel me to write this book. Had I not received a phone call from Meredith that evening, I wouldn't have given a second thought to anything that happened earlier that day. When I told my story to special agent Scott Campbell from the Kansas Bureau of Investigation in January 2014, I said, "I actually thought we had a good day. The next thing I know I'm getting investigated by the KBI."

Chapter 2

The Phone Call

AFTER ABIGAIL LEFT, the evening of December 2 continued in our pattern of normalcy: cooking dinner, eating dinner, bath time, stories, bedtime. When the twins were asleep, Mike, our older son Ryan, and I settled into watch Monday Night Football—Saints versus Seahawks. I was only half-watching because the bulk of my attention was on Thomas's Christmas stocking. We were settled in the living room about 8:15 p.m. when my phone rang. It was Meredith, which definitely wasn't normal. She seldom called me, usually choosing to text, and she rarely contacted me at night. The game was so loud that I excused myself to our bedroom to hear her better.

I perched on the edge of the bed and listened as Meredith blurted, "I'm on my way to the emergency room with Abigail because her arm is hard and stiff." This is when I started having two conversations simultaneously: the one I was having with Meredith and the one I was having with myself inside of my head.

"Oh no!" *Why is she telling me this?*

Meredith continued, "Did anything happen at your house? She was cranky when I put her coat on to leave." *Oh, that's why she's telling me this.* Meredith wasn't yelling, but it was an accusatory statement and her tone immediately put me on the defensive. She didn't directly say, "My child is injured and it happened at your house," but her implication was obvious.

I did recall Abigail reacting atypically when Meredith moved to put her coat on. Abigail would sometimes whine a little when Meredith arrived, but that afternoon she cried out and plopped down on the floor when Meredith tried to put her arm in a sleeve. Abigail didn't normally throw those mini tantrums. *Does that mean her arm was already injured when she left? How weird. She didn't act like she was injured.*

I scrolled through the mental images of our day and landed on pushing through the gate when we arrived back from our outing, because it was the most physical thing that happened that day. *I was holding her when I pushed through the gate. She was crying. Should I tell Meredith about the baby gate? Of course I should.* I described it to Meredith just like I would describe it later to Daniel Holland in my first interview.

As we talked about the gate, my mind started to churn over the facts I had at hand. *Meredith says Abigail's arm is hard and stiff. It's serious enough that she's taking her to the ER at 8:30 p.m. She says it happened with me. But how could it have happened here? Nothing happened at my house. Nothing ever happens at my house.*

Then I thought about something else that occurred during our day—the thing I would lie about to Meredith, my husband, my family, my friends, and the police—and all hell broke loose inside my brain. *Did that break her arm? That couldn't possibly have broken her arm. I would have known, right? But did it? Is that why her arm is hard and stiff and Meredith is taking her to the emergency room!? How could it be that? But oh my god that must be it!*

I had offered the gate incident to Meredith in full detail, but on this I recoiled. There was one specific thing about this event that, coupled with Meredith's decision that Abigail was injured at my house, made me sure that I was responsible. *Don't tell her that.* And so I didn't. I knew how Abigail's arm came to be injured, but I lied and said I didn't. We concluded the call as Meredith neared the hospital, and I walked back to the football game, my mind in a very different place from a few minutes before.

Mike and Ryan were still watching the game, oblivious to what had just transpired in the bedroom. I told Mike, "That was Meredith. She's taking Abigail to the hospital. She said Abigail's arm felt hard and stiff while they were giving her a bath." And then, because I have a tendency towards theatrical exaggerations of emotion, I burst out, "I'm going to prison!"

Mike was used to my communication style by now, but he was obviously—and justifiably—confused by my panic. From his vantage point, I had been sewing a Christmas stocking, left the room to take a phone call, and now was convinced I had a future as an inmate. He would have been better oriented to my alarm if he knew what I had just realized I'd done, but there was no way I was telling him. If he knew, he would never let me lie about it.

Puzzled, he said, "What are you talking about?"

I threw myself into the living room chair and repeated my conversation with Meredith, making sure to include more lamentations about how much trouble I was in and how bad the situation was.

Mike calmly said, "We need to talk about this." He ushered me down the hallway to our bedroom while Ryan stayed behind and continued watching the game, seemingly unperturbed by my distress. "Tell me about your day with the kids," he said once he closed the door. "Start at the beginning."

I began when Steve brought Abigail over and went step-by-step through our day, including stumbling through the gate. When I finished, we looked at each other quizzically until Mike said, "Why would any of that hurt her arm?" We agreed that nothing I had described—which I knew wasn't everything that happened—would have injured her.

"But something hurt her arm, because Meredith said her arm is hurt and it happened here."

"Sounds like those fucking people need to figure out what happened at their house," he said matter-of-factly and then left the room. Mike walked back to the living room to finish watching the football game, thinking that this incident was over and done. But on my end, shame started creeping in. Not only was I worried about potentially having injured a child, but I had also just lied to my husband.

Back in the living room, I settled somewhat when Ryan pointed out that Meredith might be overly anxious, and I did wonder if perhaps Meredith was exaggerating the condition of Abigail's arm. Following the game, we went to bed, where Mike would later claim he "slept like a baby" while I stared at the ceiling, unable to calm my racing heart and mind.

❧

The next morning, I could barely choke down my breakfast because my stomach was in knots. I managed to go through the morning routine and get Ryan to school without falling apart. Before 9:00 a.m., Ryan sent a text from school that read, *Abigail has a spiral fracture. Her brother just told me.* My stomach flipped.

Within minutes of Ryan's text, Meredith called me and confirmed the news. My position as Abigail's caretaker had just gone from questionable to downright suspect. I knew from work experience that spiral fractures always raise the red flag of suspected child abuse. Not only had I broken Abigail's arm, but now the term *abuse* was attached to what I had done.

Meredith explained, "I don't know how it happened. I spoke with a friend who said kids can break their arm if it gets caught in the crib the wrong way." I gave a half-hearted acknowledgment of this as a possibility, but I knew what had really happened. And still a deep hesitation cautioned me to stay quiet.

Feeling her out, I asked, "Is Abigail going to come over today?" Meredith said no and added that investigators would be calling me.

The fact that Meredith wasn't bringing Abigail back to my house confirmed that the injury likely occurred when she was with me. Standard procedure is to instruct nonoffending caregivers to keep the child away from an alleged perpetrator while the investigation is ongoing. I also wasn't surprised that investigators would be contacting me. Once I heard the words *spiral fracture* the next word that went through my head was *investigation*.

Despite her subtle accusations the night before, Meredith didn't sound upset in this conversation. Her speech was a little halting, and she paused before she spoke or answered questions. I wondered if maybe the phone call was being recorded. Investigators sometimes record phone calls to get the suspect to say something incriminating.

We ended the phone call after chatting about how Abigail was doing. After I hung up, I stood in my kitchen thinking, *Now what?* I didn't want to call a lawyer, because wouldn't that just make me look guilty? And I *wasn't* guilty—or at least, I hadn't done anything abusive.

The days following were dark and lonely. Not only did I think I had broken a child's arm, but I couldn't talk to anyone about it. I didn't even tell Mike. I didn't want to put him in an awkward position by telling him what I had done. Telling the police the truth was a terrible idea, but I also knew Mike would never encourage me to lie about it.

I'm a direct communicator and I've never been the kind of person to intentionally lie. When I lied to the police, I surprised myself as much as anyone. So why did I do it?

My first instinct was self-preservation. I had been informed that a child was injured, and I didn't want to be in trouble for having caused it. I didn't want any accusations against me to embarrass Ryan, who attended school with the Holders' son in our small town. Another reason for my lie was less concrete and more intuitive. Something about the whole situation felt off to me from the outset. When Meredith called me en route to the hospital, intuition took over and said, *Don't tell her anything.* I couldn't put my finger on it at the time of the phone call or for several weeks afterwards, but something was out of alignment. I thought our day was as normal as you could get, and then out of the blue I learned that Abigail was going to the emergency room for something her mother indicated was my fault. Going back to my mindset during this time is challenging because of everything that came next, but looking back I can see that some part of myself instinctively knew what was coming and was trying to save me from it.

When I was told that Abigail's injury was a spiral fracture, I added another layer to my decision: first-hand experience with the inner workings of the child welfare system. My overriding fear was that I would tell investigators what happened and, not believing my story, they would accuse me of doing something else. This might seem paranoid, but working within the system forever changed how I see Child Protective Services (CPS) investigations. Nobody knows how a child abuse investigation can go off the rails like somebody who used to be a CPS social worker. Once they're investigating you, you don't control the narrative anymore.

❦

I never aspired to work at the Department for Children and Families[1] (DCF) doing child abuse investigations for the State of Kansas. I participated in a practicum my senior year of college at

---

1 At the time I worked for social services, the department was called the Department of Social and Rehabilitation services (SRS) but later changed to its current name, the Department for Children and Families (DCF). For consistency's sake, I'll be using its current name throughout this book.

the University of Kansas to obtain my degree in social welfare, and the university placed me at DCF. My practicum resulted in a ten-year employment with the State of Kansas that ushered me into an underworld full of drugs, mental illness, sexual depravity, and poverty. Prior to working for the State, I didn't know there were people on this earth who lived how some of my clients did. Even after leaving DCF, I couldn't forget they were still out there.

One of the best parts of my job was my co-workers. The Douglas County DCF office was an extremely family-friendly place to work, and we had each other for support on the bad days. Accurately conveying the trials and tribulations of CPS to an outsider is hard because the work is almost indescribable, but a fellow CPS worker will always get it. I had a great deal of respect for other social workers within my agency, but I wasn't blind to how poor work product can negatively impact the lives of families, even if the professionals have the best intentions. Facts are facts, but the outcome of a child abuse case depends quite a bit on how the assigned social worker interprets those facts. Everything is subjective. In any situation that involves real people and judgment calls, the outcome will not always be fair or correct.

A co-worker once stopped by my cubicle and mentioned that she just placed a client on the Child Abuse Registry for dangling his son over a banister while roughhousing. I was taken aback by this decision because Mike had dangled Ryan over our own banister in the recent past while they were playing around. Beyond that, two of my male friends had done the same thing to Ryan years earlier. I don't know what it is about men, boys, and bannisters, but nothing about either situation presented itself as abusive to me. It probably wasn't the best decision-making, but I didn't think it warranted placement on the Registry. I wouldn't have made that decision had it been my case, but it wasn't my case.

You hear about failures in CPS when a child dies and it makes the news, but there are many ways that don't involve a death where bad decision-making can negatively impact families. Not every decision made by CPS workers changes the trajectory of someone's life, but some do. Social workers decide which children get to stay in their homes and which don't, which actions are abusive and which aren't, who needs to change their behavior and who doesn't. CPS decisions can be life-altering but, unfortunately—and sometimes tragically—all decisions made by social workers are completely subjective. I knew I didn't want someone else to decide if I acted in an abusive way towards Abigail. I lived the day, and I knew I hadn't.

⁂

The personality of the DCF social worker isn't the only factor that affects a case. The child welfare system consists of contractors who provide in-home services, foster care workers, therapists, school staff, police officers, judges, and attorneys. I could have a certain perspective on a client, but the opinion of another individual from a different agency could take the case in a completely different direction.

I removed two young children from their mother because her use of meth was not conducive to good parenting. As is common with meth addicts, this woman was aggressive and erratic in any meeting I had with her prior to the removal. While the children were in foster care, I attended a meeting involving the client and her foster care workers. After a few minutes, it became apparent that the foster care workers had determined that the mother wasn't the problem. Instead, they had determined that *I* was the problem. When I tried to voice my concerns regarding the mother's parenting, the foster care workers interrupted me and wouldn't let me continue. Maybe they were right and I had judged the mom too harshly, or maybe I was right that the client had successfully manipulated the foster care workers. What I know is that her workers soon recommended to the court that the mother regain custody of her kids. She moved out of state and not much later had her kids removed again. I wondered how it might have been different for the children had the Kansas foster care workers held the mother accountable in the beginning.

The subjectivity within the system could be so consequential that later in my career I would advise people to hire a private attorney or locate private services if they had the means, so that they wouldn't be at the mercy of the system. In the hallway outside of court, an attorney once pulled me aside and asked, "Do you mind if I ask you why you told my clients to obtain their own attorney and stay away from your agency?"

I replied, "Your clients want their granddaughter to be safe and they want the State of Kansas to provide that safety. But your clients aren't going to be able to pick which worker is assigned to their case or what decisions that person will make regarding their grandchild. I believe if a family can solve their own problems instead of having the State in their business, then they need to do that and keep us out of it."

Sometimes I felt the State was justified in intervening. Certain people leave you with absolutely no choice. But if you have the means to avoid becoming entangled with the State of Kansas, it's in your best interest to do that.

When Meredith indicated in our phone call that investigators would be contacting me, I assumed, correctly, that investigators meant not only a CPS social worker but also the police. The majority of cases I was assigned involved allegations that were not criminal offenses, so I worked them by myself. When a case involved an allegation that could potentially be a crime, however, such as a child with a spiral fracture, we referred the report to the police and investigated it alongside them.

Since these events started unfolding in 2013 and 2014, law

enforcement has become a hot-button issue. Mike has been employed as a police officer at the Lawrence Kansas Police Department since 1998 and has served as a detective since 2011. In addition to my husband, my brother-in-law is a cop, their cousin works in law enforcement and is married to a cop, and my husband's friends are cops. Having a personal relationship with a police officer makes the entire profession look different.

While at DCF, I got along well with law enforcement officers, or at least I like to think I did. I liked almost all of them on a personal level. A well-intentioned police officer can be a welcome sight when you have lost your ability to cope. I also acknowledge that being fed a constant diet of negativity, potential and actualized violence, verbal harassment, misplaced aggression, and uncontrolled anger would wear on a person. A bad day for a police officer is a lot different from a bad day for a civilian, and day after day of that nonsense could turn an otherwise pleasant officer into a bit of a curmudgeon. No matter how ugly my days are, they never involve looking at the unfiltered aftermath of a suicide or murder.

Some people might assume that I regard officers as more friend than foe, but it's more complicated than that. I have respect for a group of people who sacrifice their lives for the betterment of society, but while working at DCF I came to view the police in the same way I viewed social workers and community members within the child welfare system. The personality, temperament, life experiences, and competence of police officers factor into their decision-making and affect the outcome of the case just as it does for everybody else. Law enforcement is a noble profession in theory, but that doesn't mean that every person who works in the law enforcement profession is noble. Anybody who deals with the police as much as I have knows that talking to them can sometimes be risky. When I later decided to tell my whole story to investigators, three people advised that I shouldn't talk to the cops without a lawyer. Two of those people were police officers. Even the *police* know you shouldn't always talk to the police.

My marriage to a police officer and regular interaction with the police at my job helped me see police officers for who they are: people. They're people like everybody else. We cannot assume that individuals will never make a mistake simply because of the title or job they hold. That idealization is unfair to officers and unfair to society. We cannot expect superhuman actions from people who are simply human.

In December 2013, I knew enough about police officers to not to be afraid of them, but I also knew enough to fear what might happen if I told them everything.

The subjectivity of the system became part of my own worldview. Even though by December 2013 I had been unemployed for two years, I was still carrying all these stories and experiences around when Meredith called to tell me Abigail was injured. That phone call instantly accessed the part of me that was still a social worker. It's not that I didn't trust the system at all; rather, I didn't trust the system all of the time. I didn't have full faith that I would be treated fairly, or that my actions would be interpreted correctly, or that whoever was assigned my case would get it right. I had enough experience to know that I might get excellent social workers and officers who would do an exceptional job—or I might not. Was I going to be assigned someone with common sense and objectivity? Or was I going to be assigned someone who was burned out and incompetent? Was I going to get someone with experience or a newbie? I didn't want to roll the dice. It wasn't in my best interest to put myself at the mercy of the child welfare system, and so I lied.

Chapter 3

The Search Warrant

AS I DROVE the five blocks from the police department to my house after my initial interview, I listed my transgressions to date. Breaking the arm of an innocent child. *Check.* Lying to her parents to save my own hide. *Check.* Lying to the father of my own children and allowing him to think Abigail's parents were likely responsible. *Check.* Lying to a police officer to avoid incarceration. *Check.* It had only been three days, but I was building quite the criminal résumé, and I was planning to soon add a whopper to my repertoire: squirming on the hot seat of a polygraph exam.

I listened to the radio as I drove, a little amped up from the interview but pleased enough with my performance that I hummed along like I usually do. Mike had taken a long lunch to stay home with the kids and I needed to get back so he could leave for work. When I entered the house, Mike was calmly waiting for me.

"How was it?"

I replied, "I'm glad it's over. Holland didn't ask a lot of questions. He just had me tell him what happened, so I told him about my day. It was way easier than I thought it would be, but then at the end he asked me to take a polygraph. That surprised me. What do you think that means?"

Mike, unaware of my guilt but sensing my apprehension and seeking to reassure me, said, "It won't be a big deal. The KBI is big into the polygraphs. They probably have to give so many polygraphs per year to keep up their certification. Just take it and get it over with."

While my screeching anxiety had lessened to a dull thud in my brain since the interview, I now turned my attention to obsessing about how I was going to do on the polygraph. Mike and I were in the living room one evening after Thomas and Joseph were asleep. I was still having trouble understanding spiral fractures and how that would translate to my polygraph, and I thought Mike might be able to give me some helpful information.

Casually I said, "I'm confused about what causes a spiral fracture. How do they happen?"

Still not aware that I caused the injury, Mike said, "It will be easier if I demonstrate it." He stood up and acted like he was holding the hand of a young child standing on the ground. Then he demonstrated a violent and aggressive yanking and twisting motion with his arm that was, quite frankly, appalling.

Mike's reenactment not only gave me a disturbing visual of what happens to a child during a spiral fracture, but also a horrible realization of what Daniel Holland likely thought I did. I thought, *I didn't do that! I didn't do anything even remotely close to that, but people will think I did because she has a spiral fracture.*

As I endlessly ruminated on what I had done, what people were going to think I did, and what the polygraph would be like, my outward life went on as normal. The kids and I went on our outings as usual—walks in the wood, visits to the aquarium—without incident, but one social gathering was a major source of anxiety: Ryan's basketball games. Ryan and the Holders' oldest son, Jared, played on the same team. Seeing Steve and Meredith was inevitable.

Prior to the first basketball game after Abigail's ER visit, Mike and I mapped out our plan of action. We intended to sit close enough to the Holders to not appear avoidant, but far enough away that we wouldn't have to talk to them. Having a conversation with them about her injury—or anything, really—was the last thing I wanted to do. Our plan was foiled as soon as we entered the opposing team's gym because the only available seating was right where Steve was already sitting. Not entirely sure how to start this conversation, I decided to just dive right in. Steve and I had always laughed with each other, so as Mike and I passed by him on the way to our seat, I lightheartedly said, "Hi, Steve. Gee, I'm sorry we're getting investigated by the KBI and I have to take a polygraph." Adopting the same joking tone, he smiled and replied, "Hey, I know."

The next few games were home games, which made our plan to sit separately from the Holders a little bit easier because of the gym layout. During one game, Meredith and Abigail sought us out. Coming up behind us as we sat focused on the game, Meredith said, "We haven't seen you in a while!" Her tone was so friendly that it was clear she wasn't upset with me, but her being so close made my skin crawl. We talked about how Abigail's arm was healing and her doctor's appointment while I avoided eye contact by focusing on the game.

Before walking back to her seat, Meredith suggested, "Maybe we can come over one day and play so the kids can get together." I muttered something agreeable and vague, though I had absolutely no intention of agreeing to any playdates. Between games, Meredith also sent text messages to check in, one of which said, *After this is over will you still watch Abigail?* I deflected the questions and offers the best I could. I didn't want to hang out with Meredith because I felt guilty for breaking her daughter's arm and lying about it. I knew I was guilty (and the police appeared to agree with me), but Mike was sure of my innocence, and Abigail's family didn't seem bothered by any of it.

The polygraph was scheduled for the afternoon of December 10, 2013. The boys and I spent the morning at a reading of a children's book—*The Pillow Fairy*—at a local party shop. The happy balloons were a sharp contrast to how I felt inside. I had joked with Steve about the polygraph, but I didn't think any of this was funny at all. I felt backed into a corner. If the polygraph administrator asked if I did something intentionally or out of anger to hurt her, I could answer that truthfully with a *no*. But if they asked me any question that put me in a position to lie about what I had done, I envisioned a flare shooting out of the machine with flashing lights, sirens sounding, and a deep voice repeatedly shouting the word, "GUILTY!" over the intercom. How was I going to explain that?

The reading only took thirty minutes, and I needed something else to occupy my time so I wouldn't worry so much. We opted to go bowling. While the kids took turns hauling enormous bowling balls up to the dinosaur-shaped ramp (all while wearing butterfly wing-shaped balloons on their backs), Holland called to tell me that the polygraph couldn't happen that afternoon because the agent who would be administering it couldn't make it. Instead of feeling relief that I wouldn't have to do it that day, I was overwhelmed that it was rescheduled. I wanted to get it over with. I had been keeping it together on the outside, but my stress level was reaching a breaking point.

Why did I even agree to participate in the polygraph? What was I going to accomplish by failing a test and making officers think I abused Abigail? The Holders didn't seem to care that I was being investigated, and the KBI wasn't even concerned enough to keep the appointment. Driving home from the bowling alley with the kids babbling to each other in the back, I suddenly realized that the polygraph was voluntary. Holland never said I had to take it and refusing it seemed like a solution that would solve all my problems. No polygraph meant that I could keep lying and nobody would find out about it. I ran it by Mike and a friend, and both affirmed that backing out was smart and okay. Not spending a lot of time thinking about the potential long-term ramifications of this decision, I cancelled the polygraph.

When I told Meredith that I cancelled the test, she responded, without suspicion or hostility in her voice, "They aren't even admissible in court." This was not the response I was expecting, but it definitely made it easier on me. She seemed perfectly understanding of my decision.

❧

On December 16, Mike was sitting at his desk looking at the dispatch screen that shows all ongoing police and fire calls. He froze when our address popped up on the call log with the words *Search Warrant* next to it. Knowing that he wasn't allowed to open any call logs that pertained to him personally, he got up from his desk and walked to his captain's office, who already knew of the ongoing investigation.

Mike stood in the doorway and said, "Something is going on at my house." He alerted his boss to what he had read on the screen.

His supervisor replied, "Don't worry about it. It's probably not a big deal."

Not convinced, Mike walked back to his desk and thought through his options. He couldn't alert me to the search warrant because that would be interfering in an investigation, which could get him fired. Losing his job was not going to help anyone, so he decided to call me and act like he was checking in just to see if I knew anything yet.

Completely clueless as to what was transpiring and thinking nothing of a daily check-in, I picked up the phone when it rang and said, "Hey, what's up?"

"Not much. How's your day going?"

"Good so far. Your mom is coming over in a few minutes to stay with the boys while they nap so I can run errands."

"How are the kids?"

"They're okay. We've had a good day so far. I just put them down for a nap, and they fell asleep fast so they must have been tired. Are you going to be home on time?"

"Yes, I should be."

Our conversation was quick. After hanging up, Mike helplessly stared at his computer screen with a sense of impending doom while whatever was about to happen to me unfolded at our house.

At home, I had just finished putting my shoes on when there was a knock at the door. I opened it expecting to see my mother-in-law, Marsha. Instead, Daniel Holland and Officer Victor Lockhart from the Eudora Police Department were standing on the other side. Surprised doesn't even begin to describe my feelings.

My dog, Winston—who alerts us to any and all possible danger, including barking maniacally at neighbors entering their own homes—somehow missed that the individuals standing on our doorstep were a massive threat to me, instead taking the opportunity to have his ears rubbed. Holland obliged and asked, "What kind of dog is this?"

I didn't know why Holland was standing on my steps asking about my dog, but I answered the question anyway. "He's a vizsla."

Holland continued petting Winston while Lockhart stood beside him showing all the signs of awkward discomfort. Finally, because Holland wasn't saying anything at all beyond cooing at my dog, I asked, "Why are you here?"

Holland stopped petting Winston, stood up, and answered, "I have a search warrant for your phone."

Immediately I thought, *I am dead. Like, right now I am dying,* and then I began contemplating what to do next. *Should I invite them in? Do we stand outside? I don't want these people in my house, but this is embarrassing and I don't want my neighbors to see.* My house is a bilevel and our entryway couldn't accommodate all three of us. I had no choice but to invite them all the way into my home.

Standing in the middle of my living room with Holland and Lockhart, I couldn't keep the stress out of my voice. "I told you that you could look through my phone when I talked to you. You didn't have to get a warrant and take it like this. I would have given it to you."

As Holland began reading the search warrant to me, I heard a light knock on the door and Marsha, whom I was expecting earlier, walked in. *How much worse can this get?* I was not only under siege by the police, but now my mother-in-law, who was already aware of the investigation, was bearing witness to it. I explained, "This is the police officer investigating the case. He's here with a search warrant for my phone." Marsha acknowledged this but said little and sat down quietly on the couch.

As Marsha watched, Holland finished reading me the search warrant and, having no choice in the matter, I begrudgingly handed him my phone. Before I did so, I said, "I'm going to text Mike to tell him what's happening." I could see the hesitation in Holland's body while he simply said, "Oh, no. . . ." Immediately I understood that I wasn't allowed to use the phone now that he had legal possession of it.

There was no extensive small talk after Holland took my phone. He thanked me, and then he and Lockhart walked out of my home. I watched from the window as they quickly walked side-by-side all the way down my street and around the corner. I realized they didn't park the patrol car in front of the house because they didn't want to embarrass Mike. That may have been a kindness towards my husband, but it did nothing to improve their standing with me. Any ambiguous feelings I may have had towards Holland had vanished. I now understood very clearly that he was an adversary.

I used Marsha's phone to call Mike to tell him what happened.

"Daniel Holland just came over and took my phone with a search warrant."

Still at work and unable to tell me that he had seen it come across the call log, Mike only said, "What?"

I was so rattled that I kept babbling, "I would have given it to him a long time ago! He didn't have to take it like that. I would have given it him without a warrant because there's nothing on it. Do you think I'm getting it back?"

The seizure of my phone is when Mike and I came to understand the case in vastly different ways. I felt attacked and unsettled by Holland showing up unannounced and taking my property, but I didn't view the seizure of my phone as something that could hurt me because I knew there wasn't anything incriminating on it. I didn't care if Holland looked through it. He could have gone through my entire house and all my possessions and I wouldn't have cared, because I knew he wasn't going to find anything. All Holland could determine by taking my phone is that I read a lot of sewing blogs. Just like with everything else about this case, I responded to the search warrant by compartmentalizing. I left Marsha at home with the kids and drove to Walmart, where I stumbled through the aisles buying toothpaste and laundry detergent.

Mike saw the seizure of my phone in a completely different way. While I was at Walmart, Mike drove home, where he found the copy of the search warrant I had left on our secretary. At the top it described the crime that was being investigated: *Aggravated Battery and Child Abuse*. As he read those words he said aloud, "They're trying to throw her in prison."

I didn't understand the severity of Holland's actions in a legal sense, but Mike did. Although he still didn't know that I had broken Abigail's arm, Mike was painfully aware of police procedure and what the judge's signature on the warrant actually meant. Now it wasn't just Daniel Holland who thought I had abused a child—a judge also believed there was probable cause that a crime occurred. Mike understood this to be the standard for filing charges. From Mike's vantage point, the police didn't think what happened was an accident, because you don't get a search warrant for an accidental injury, and the next time Holland visited our house it could be with a warrant for my arrest. Mike also knew well the penalty for level-4 aggravated battery: a minimum of thirty-six months in prison no matter your criminal record. I understood what could happen—that I might be arrested at some point—but I was under such stress that I also didn't *really* understand what could happen. So while I was thinking, *I guess maybe I'll be going to jail?* Mike was thinking, *But no really, she's probably going to jail.*

From an investigative standpoint, I think Holland was right to arrive at my house unannounced. As part of my job at the State, I routinely arrived at residences without calling first because the element of surprise was the whole point. Surprising people allows them less time to cover their tracks or make plans. But two things about the search warrant bothered me greatly, and not just for myself.

First, this is a portion of what Holland wrote in the search warrant regarding the polygraph exam:

> On today's date, AFFIANT has been made aware from other law enforcement assisting in the investigation that VERBANIC has exchanged text messages with Abigail's mother, Meredith, regarding the circumstances of the ongoing investigation to the extent of at least discussing requests that she submit to a polygraph exam, which VERBANIC had earlier been offered and declined to accept.

When I made the move to decline to take the polygraph, Holland's next move was strategic: present an affidavit to a judge requesting seizure of my phone. Holland didn't request a search warrant for my phone immediately after I said I had pictures on it in my initial interview. He didn't accept my phone when I offered it voluntarily. Only when I refused the polygraph did Daniel Holland seize my phone. Now I know that polygraphs are voluntary except that if you decline, the police will think you're guilty. So if you want to prove your innocence, you have to take the polygraph. In short, polygraphs are voluntarily mandatory.

Reading further through the affidavit, Holland states his reason for confiscating my phone:

> AFFIANT's experience has been that people who have committed criminal acts associated with the circumstances of this investigation, as well as others, will frequently contact people familiar to them to seek advice on how to deal with the situation, to get information about how to conceal their actions or to report the acts, either in phone conversations or via text messages, people will sometimes access websites that they believe will help explain the conduct and phones can provide tagging information as to time and location of the phone that is associated with the person.

To obtain my phone, all Holland had to tell the judge was that in his experience people who commit crimes talk about it with their friends or search Google for how to cover it up. He didn't have to cite a specific reason for knowing that I did this (such as somebody telling him that I did). He had no real basis for believing that I did those things other than his experience with other criminals. His reasoning said, *I have decided that Andrea is guilty and would like to go on a fishing expedition,* and the judge signed the document that enabled him to rifle through my personal property.

I would later gain access to a report detailing what the KBI located on my phone, which, as I suspected, was absolutely nothing. When Daniel Holland took my phone, he did so with the desire to gather evidence to use against me. Instead, he gathered evidence that *helped* me—or at least it would have if anybody had bothered to pay attention to it.

⚘

The holidays came and went. I tried to enjoy them, but it was hard. As a diversion, I rehearsed "Jingle Bells" with Joseph, him on the tambourine and me on the bongo drums, but my heart wasn't in it.

On December 29, 2013, on her own volition, Meredith copied me on an email she sent to Daniel Holland stating that she didn't think that I broke Abigail's arm. She wrote,

> We have a long history and I have NEVER seen anything at all that might indicate she is an abusive person, in fact her actions and responses to her children and the children of other people indicate the contrary. She is a loving, thoughtful, and proactive parent. I really feel that she did NOT harm my child. I have observed her with her own children in a variety of settings over the years, and as you can see by reviewing the pictures and videos of the interactions between Abigail and her family on her phone, she is a super awesome mother and caregiver.

The email was a nice gesture, but I hated it. I felt guilt and shame that she sent the email without knowing that I actually did break her child's arm. The only reply I could muster was, "Thank you for saying this, but you don't need to stick up for me."

On January 3, 2014, one of my friends called and said, "Daniel Holland stopped by my house today unannounced to ask me about you. Oh my god, my house was so dirty because I hadn't cleaned up after lunch yet, but he was nice about it. I mean, there were Cheerios all over the floor but he said he has kids too so he wasn't worried about it."

Within minutes, another friend texted, *Holland just came to my house to ask me about you. He seems harmless.*

I called Mike about it, who said, "Holland also stopped by my work today. I didn't want to tell you about it until I got home in case it worried you. I didn't want you to be worrying at home by yourself." They all defended me to Holland, which made me feel worse because they didn't know I was guilty.

On January 7, I called Meredith and told her that I didn't think it was appropriate for me to continue sitting on the board of directors of her business (which I'd served on since October 2013) with the investigation ongoing.

She said, "That's probably for the best." I could hear stress and annoyance in her voice that hadn't been there in any of our previous conversations.

Concerned, I asked, "Are you okay?"

She replied, "No. Daniel Holland asked me and Steve to take polygraphs since you aren't taking one."

I said I was sorry that they would have to go through this, and we quickly ended the phone call. This new development changed things for me—dramatically.

Up to this point, I was well aware that I was the main suspect. In fact, it was painfully obvious to me that I was the *only* suspect. Lying to save yourself and lying to get someone else in trouble are two very different things, at least in my world. I could tolerate lying if it meant getting myself out of trouble for something I did, but I couldn't tolerate lying if it meant that someone else would have to suffer. The gig was up. It was time to tell people what I had done, and the first person on my list was Mike.

After the kids were in bed, I said, "I have to tell you something bad." I sat on the couch while Mike sat across the room in the chair. All the stress and shame I had kept under wraps over the last weeks collided in this one moment and rendered me incapable of speaking. I rocked back and forth sobbing while Mike sat completely still, the panicked look in his eyes belying the forced smile plastered on his face.

After multiple moments, I finally sputtered through tears, "I lied. I've lied the whole time. I've known since Meredith's first phone call that I broke Abigail's arm. But I didn't mean to! I didn't even know I did until Meredith called!"

Still sitting on the chair, Mike held up a hand and said, "Okay, slow down. Tell me what happened."

"Everything happened that day just like I said it did—except for one thing. I pushed through the baby gate when we came home, dropped all the stuff I was carrying on the floor and . . . " The next few moments were hard as I explained in detail what had happened at our house that day and why I had lied about it. "I don't even know how something like that would cause a spiral fracture, but it's the only thing that could have because there was the pop."

When I was finished, Mike came over to where I sat on the couch and knelt down in front of me. Whenever somebody screwed up, he does this thing where he's really nice about it, which usually ends up making you feel way worse. This confession was no different. He said, "It's okay. I understand how this happened. It's all going to be all right."

Anguished for what I was putting him through, I sobbed, "I'm so sorry. You can divorce me if you want to."

He smiled a little and replied, "I'm not going to divorce you. We'll get through this."

Now that I knew Holland had turned his attention to the Holders, I immediately knew that I would have to tell him what I had done.

Sitting together on the couch, I told Mike, "I have to tell Holland. Keeping this secret has been too hard and I can't live like this anymore."

Mike said, "I know lying is a hard thing for you to do. I understand why you want to tell him. I support you in that."

"I know he's probably going to arrest me, but I'm going to have to take that chance. It's not fair to Steve and Meredith for me not to say anything. Plus, they need to know what happened to their child. I'm going to call him tomorrow. I just want to get it over with. Mike, I'm so sorry."

He put his arm around me and said, "It's okay. We're going to get through this."

I added, "And one more thing. I know most people would call a lawyer, but I'm not going to do that. A lawyer is going to tell me not to talk to Holland, but the not telling is the thing that has been eating me alive. I don't want a lawyer to get me out of trouble. I did something wrong and it's on me to take responsibility for that." Mike knew what talking to the police was going to get me—a stint in the slammer—but he also knew how I operate. Once I've made my mind up about something, it's a done deal. No one, not even Mike, could have talked me out of this one. After we talked and I decided on my plan, I went to bed and slept better than I had in weeks.

Before I spoke to Holland, I wanted to explain things to Meredith and Steve because I felt I owed them an explanation more than I owed Holland one. I wasn't sure what would happen to me once I spoke with Holland, but I was prepared to not be allowed to contact the Holder family afterward.

The morning after my confession to Mike I went down to our basement and called Meredith, my mind and body in a weird emotional state that was a mash-up of dread and relief. Mike knew what I was going to say, but I was so ashamed that I didn't want him to hear me. When she answered, I started right in. "I'm sorry to call you out of the blue like this, but I have to tell you something about Abigail's arm. I know how it was broken. I think I broke her arm when she was at my house that day. I didn't realize it was broken when it happened, and I promise it wasn't intentional. I'm so sorry that I've lied all this time."

Sounding only mildly exasperated, she said, "I wish you had told me this sooner."

"Meredith, I'm so sorry. I know I should have said something earlier."

Instead of becoming angry and asking me what happened to her child, which is what I expected, she said, "I never understood why they thought it was you. Even at the hospital, the officer said right away, 'Oh, so this happened at your babysitter's house.' I don't know why he decided that so early in the investigation. Abigail never really showed any signs of being injured in the evening at our house. She only ever cried when somebody touched her arm. She even helped me sort laundry."

"I'm going to call Daniel Holland and tell him what I did, but I want to tell you first. I want you to hear it from me. Can we set up a time to meet so I can tell you and Steve together?"

She paused and then said, "Let me call Steve and tell him this. I'll tell him you want to meet and then I'll call you back." And then, almost as an afterthought, she said, "I forgive you, but I wish you had told me sooner."

I was extremely anxious but also so relieved to be starting the process. To kill time and do something besides stare at my phone waiting for it to ring, I took Winston for a walk. While I was walking, Meredith texted me.

I talked to Steve. We have decided it's not a good idea to meet with you. We think it's in your best interest to talk to Daniel Holland.

Taking the hint that she didn't want much more from me, I only replied, *I understand.*

I was disappointed that they didn't want to meet with me, but I understood why. If someone called me to say they had lied for five weeks about breaking my baby's arm, I probably wouldn't want to talk to them either.

Around noon on the same day, again from the basement, I called Holland. I had kept it together when talking with Meredith, but the tears started again when he picked up. I said, "It's Andrea Verbanic. I'm ready to be completely honest. I know how Abigail's arm was broken. I'm so sorry that I've wasted your time. Will you meet with me so I can tell you what happened?"

To his credit, Holland was kind. He said, "Hey, it's all good. I'm glad you called. I'm in some interviews right now but I can meet with you around 3:00 p.m. Does that work?"

A couple hours later, I drove to the Eudora Police Department to confess.

Chapter 4

The Confession

I ADMIT TO being afraid of my job when I started working for DCF. I wasn't afraid of certain aspects of my job or specific people. I was afraid of the whole thing from start to finish. I wanted to run and hide the first time I pulled up to a client's house with another social worker, because who in their right mind agrees to walk up to complete strangers and ask them if they beat their kid? It felt like insanity. Over time, though, all the abnormal aspects of my job started to feel normal. The chaos of social work became a regular part of my life as I became desensitized to the dysfunction. Instead of being afraid of what clients might do to me, I started worrying that the filth was going to mess up my new shoes. When individuals were high on drugs and rocking back and forth in the hallway talking to themselves, I simply said, "Excuse me, please," and stepped around them.

I lost the anxiety but, unfortunately, I also lost some of my tenderness—a lot of it, actually. Disillusionment is a job hazard everybody falls victim to if you stick around long enough. Without a protective shell around yourself, the job is too much, and the troublesome clients—many of whom can smell fear—tend to prey upon the weak. If you don't have your guard up, you'll burn out and eventually quit. If too many people do that, the system winds up with a unit full of frontline social workers who have limited experience dealing with hard cases of abuse. Experience matters, but with experience also comes a fair dose of cynicism.

As I worked more cases, I also developed an incredibly perverse sense of humor and an ability to laugh at any misfortune, even if that misfortune was in no way funny. People outside the system would be appalled if they heard how CPS workers talk about their cases, but it's not born of insensitivity—it's a matter of emotional survival. Irreverent humor is how CPS workers deal with the steady stream of negativity, because nobody reports good behavior to the child abuse hotline. Many of my clients were toxic and dysfunctional—which is why they were clients.

Becoming a good social worker is about becoming experienced, but not so experienced that you lose touch with your humanity. You need to know enough to not be shocked by the realities of your clients' lives, but not know so much that you burn out. You need to have enough knowledge to read a situation correctly and respond to it in the right way, but not so much that you judge everybody as unredeemable. You have to know when someone needs a soft touch, and when somebody needs to be called out. You must have empathy, but if you're emotionally invested in every case, your work product suffers. It's a tough balancing act, and not one that I always succeeded at.

I was a good social worker, but some days I was better than others. Some days I felt like I bettered humanity, and other days I didn't. The client's situation had something to do with that, obviously, but so did my mood, my caseload, and what was going on in my own life. Clients might catch me at a compassionate moment when I had plenty of time to devote to their needs, or they might catch me at a time when I was juggling too many cases, or I had just been screamed at, or I hadn't eaten lunch because I had been too busy, or I just wanted to get the interview over with so I could go home.

Despite the stressors of my job, I grew to like what I did for a living, as well as many of the people I investigated. I genuinely cared about most of my clients, and I wanted to help them live a better life. I liked that every day brought something new, and I liked the nature of an investigation and assessment. Interviewing people in a systematic way and figuring out the best way to ask a question was something I enjoyed. I also enjoyed advocating for people or helping them feel a little bit better about their situation. I had several chances to apply for a supervisor position or other jobs within the agency, but I never did. I didn't want to be a supervisor because I didn't want to deal with personnel issues, and, far more important than that, I liked interacting with the clients. I was a frontline worker at heart, not a manager, and so I remained a frontline worker for ten years. I didn't enjoy every conversation I ever had, but the fun part for me was talking to people. I like stories, and every once in a while, I would find a gem.

I once met a couple at their home to speak with them about a physical abuse allegation involving their daughter. We chatted until I had all the information I needed, and then I had to address the elephant in the room: Shelves covered every wall, floor to ceiling holding row upon row of ceramic figures.

I said, "I have to ask what is on your shelves."

"They're salt and pepper shakers. We collect them."

Surprised, I asked, "How many do you have?"

"Three thousand."

My eyes bugged. "No kidding?"

They really weren't kidding. I spent close to an hour taking a tour of their living room, kitchen, and spare bedroom so they could show me their collection. Every variety of salt and pepper shaker known to mankind was in that apartment—fruits, vegetables, animals both domestic and exotic, television characters.

I had no idea that every mammal, inanimate object, and cartoon character you could ever conceive of has been crafted into a salt and pepper shaker. It was as if a traveling Smithsonian exhibit had landed in subsidized housing. A few of my co-workers wanted to see it, but I couldn't justify another visit to the residence with my entire unit in tow just to gawk.

Being a good social worker is easy when you are assigned a family that didn't abuse their child and also happens to have three thousand salt and pepper shakers in their apartment. It's harder to bring your A-game when facing individuals who have lost a significant portion of their charm.

Once I was forced to schedule an interview at 4:30 p.m. on a Friday with a family I was not working well with. I found the parents to be difficult people who complained about everything I did. To add insult to injury, they were late to the interview, which irritated me because I wanted to go home on time. When the dad walked in the interview room, he looked ruffled and had a bloody gash on his arm. He said, "Sorry I'm late. I got hit by a car on the way over here." I completely ignored what I thought was a manipulative cry for attention and instead slid the DCF informational brochure across the table and instructed him to read it. Unsurprisingly, the interview went downhill from there, and he asked to speak with my supervisor.

I walked to the office of the only supervisor still at work where other social workers were gathered and explained, "This guy is up front and wants to speak with you because he's mad at me. I'm warning you that he's upset because he got hit by a car on the way over here." It wasn't until everybody stopped talking mid-sentence and stared at me that I realized a client being hit by a car was a situation that merited a more sympathetic response—or even just *any* response.

Showing a significant lack of empathy on some cases didn't work well, but neither did having too many feelings. In my early years, I worked with an incredibly challenging teenager and her equally challenging parents. I didn't have healthy emotional boundaries and was blindsided when she and her family turned on me. After a particularly rough phone call with the mother, I took Ryan to a ceramics studio after work, and, instead of enjoying my time with him, I globbed paint on a porcelain figurine with tears rolling down my cheeks while other patrons stared at me. I never got emotionally involved with a client again after that.

Being your best self all day every day while working child abuse cases is impossible. I didn't expect the individuals assigned to Abigail's case to care about my life as much as I did. This was only their job, so why would they be as invested in me as I was?

I don't think I was a salt-and-pepper-shaker case for Daniel Holland. After the second interview, I'm pretty sure I was the guy who got hit by a car.

⮑

On January 8, 2014, I arrived at the police department in a state of nervous exhaustion, but still ready to talk. I nervously avoided the gaze of the receptionist and stood in the lobby until Holland came to fetch me. We didn't speak much as he led me down the hallway to the interview room. He had been nice on the phone earlier in the day and he was cordial enough now, but my guard was still up.

I sat down and faced the wall as I spoke, looking away from Holland, who was sitting directly to my left. I dived right in. I bypassed the play-by-play of the day and explained, "Everything I told you last time happened exactly like I told you. The morning happened like I said it did." Mechanically, I touched on a few things we did that morning—how Abigail was tired when she arrived, how I was tense at the tree festival, how Abigail was upset in the car on the way home—but I was most anxious to straighten out my lie.

I rehashed pushing through the baby gate and then, to defend myself before I got to the meat of it, I explained, "I don't know why I'm so focused on people knowing I wasn't angry that day. I think it was kind of frustrating going through the gate, but it wasn't enraging. I wasn't furious. We got through the gate and it was fine."

After holding my secret inside for weeks, everything flooded out. "After we went through the baby gate, I put all the stuff I was carrying down in the hallway. Abigail was still mad. I took her back to the spare bedroom because she was crying, and I was going to talk to her. I have done what I'm about to tell you a million times to my own kids and to her"—I took a deep breath—"I gave her a bear hug. When I hugged her, I heard a pop, but I didn't register at all that it was her arm. At the time, I thought it was her back popping. I think her arm may have been behind her back when I hugged her, but I'm not totally sure."

Now that I was talking, I couldn't stop. Talking it out like Holland was my therapist, I continued, "I think the break happened because of the positioning of her arm, but even that doesn't seem to make any sense. At the time, she didn't cry out or anything like that. After the hug, I picked her up and went downstairs to get the boys from the sandpile. Nothing was abnormal except that she didn't eat lunch. She picked at it a little but nothing like she normally did. She had been in a bad mood for a while because of the teething. I didn't think much of it, honestly. She whined when I wrapped her up for her nap, but she wasn't shrieking in pain. By nap time, nothing had gone wrong."

Still facing away from Holland, having no idea how he was receiving this information, I continued to ramble, "It didn't occur to me until after I talked to Meredith that maybe the popping I heard wasn't Abigail's back. Maybe her arm popped? But at first I didn't see how hugging Abigail could have possibly done anything. It's not like I squeezed her until she couldn't breathe.

I didn't squeeze her any harder than I've squeezed my own kids a million times. I didn't say anything to Meredith about it. The next day, Meredith said Abigail had a spiral fracture, and I know from work experience that spiral fractures are always considered abusive. But I was also thinking, 'How would that hug even cause a spiral fracture? Isn't a spiral fracture twisting?' I figured if I said anything about the hug then you would say, 'That's not consistent,' and then you would ask me what I really did."

Holland remained totally silent as I spoke, but I hadn't noticed because I was barely coming up for air as I prattled on. Figuring that I needed to acknowledge how irrational my story sounded, I said, "None of this is logical. Even the telling of it is embarrassing because it makes no sense. Lying is stupid. I don't know why I did that! I have a fear of law enforcement and DCF because I've seen people make crazy assumptions and be overly judgmental. It's all so subjective. You wind up with a judgmental cop and a judgmental social worker, and it doesn't matter what the actual story is."

Moving from the sequence of events to defending my behavior, I continued, "I don't think what I did was abusive. I wasn't mad at her. I wasn't disciplining her. I wasn't punishing her. But at the same time, I must have broken her arm when I hugged her. When I asked Mike what causes a spiral fracture, he demonstrated a yanking motion, but I didn't get mad and yank her." And now, feeling the heaviness of what I had done, I started to cry. "I feel terrible that I broke her arm. It's not like I knew I did at the time, but I figured it out later."

Having finally finished unburdening my tortured soul, I turned to face Holland. I was hoping for compassion and, if I was lucky, maybe even some sympathy. I had given him what he wanted—a confession—and so I was not prepared for the emotions clear on Holland's face: annoyance and anger. There was a pause before he spoke that gave me enough time to think, *Why is he looking at me like that? What did I do wrong? Did I say something really bad?*

Holland stared hard at me and said, "I've been doing this for twenty years. I've seen a lot. Giving someone a hug is not going to cause a spiral fracture."

Preoccupied with my fear of the system, I missed the grenade Holland had just lobbed. I replied, "Can I just say for the record that this is what happened? This is what I was afraid of. I hugged her. That's it. That's what it was."

Obviously trying to keep his annoyance in check, Holland said, "It's a spiral fracture. You have to have twisting."

"But I didn't twist her."

Becoming more annoyed, Holland said, "Giving a hug won't cause a spiral fracture. It will cause compression."

Although I had spent weeks anticipating that he wouldn't believe my story, it made me unsteady when it actually happened. I had convinced myself for weeks that Abigail's injury was my fault. Now that I finally came clean, I couldn't comprehend what Holland was telling me. Before I could process what he said, though, he took control of the interview. He continued, "What I want you to do is tell me again about your outing in Lawrence."

Why is he asking me about our trip to Lawrence? Why isn't he asking me more about the hug since that's what broke her arm? I didn't understand what the trip to Lawrence had to do with anything, but I told him about it again just like I did in the first interview. In the retelling, I said, "She stumbled and twisted a little bit when she started to fall and I had hold of her hand, but no, that wouldn't have caused a spiral fracture. I don't know why you're asking me about this. I know nothing happened on our outing. That's the God's honest truth."

From an investigative standpoint, I had evidence to back up this claim and it happened to be on my phone that Holland had in his possession. I sent the picture of the children inside Liberty

Hall—with Abigail looking perfectly content—to Meredith at 11:08 a.m. The picture on the bench outside of Liberty Hall where, again, Abigail looks just fine, came a few minutes later at 11:14 a.m. The photo of Abigail smiling on the sidewalk was sent to Meredith at 11:34 a.m. Three photographs taken in a twenty-six-minute period and at different stages of our outing seem to prove what I was telling Holland: Nothing happened. In fact, we were having a good time.

Still focused on our trip to Lawrence, Holland asked, "Where did you park? What did you do inside Liberty Hall?"

How many times is he going to ask me to describe this? I said, "Okay. I can't figure out why you keep asking. Nothing happened there, but I'll answer whatever questions you have." I described, again, our path through Liberty Hall and my own kids running away. I said, "I wasn't furious or whatever. I was more anxious than anything."

I knew going into this second interview that Holland probably wouldn't believe me, but I didn't have a clear plan for how I was going to respond when that happened. I didn't know which route he would take and how I could defend myself. *What can I say to make him understand that he's going in the wrong direction? Nothing happened on our outing. How do I bring him back to the hug?* Quickly rifling through my options, I decided to try logic. I said, "Honestly, just to defend myself, if I was making this up wouldn't I make up something that would actually cause a spiral fracture? Wouldn't it make more sense to do that? The pop was at the house with the bear hug. I can't say anything else, if it happened at my house, that's how it happened. And I have to believe it did because I heard the pop." Obviously, I reasoned that if I were inclined to invent a scenario, I wouldn't invent one nobody would believe. Therefore, the story of my hug had to be true in a "the truth is stranger than fiction" sort of way.

Holland didn't bite.

Since I wasn't giving him what he wanted—a description of a violent twisting motion—Holland became a bit more aggressive. Stringing together more words than he had in either of our interviews so far, he said, "I appreciate you giving me a call, but we're not done yet. I understand you're feeling a lot of stress. I appreciate you saying you broke Abigail's arm, but the truth is only good if it's 100 percent. You may have given her a hug, but that's not how her arm broke. Doing the right thing means to stand up when it's difficult. I'm sure it's scary. My job is to get to the truth, and I don't care what the truth is as long as it's 100 percent. I can tell you right now that a hug doesn't cause a spiral fracture."

But I am telling the truth! I am being 100 percent honest! I started to say, "This is what I'm telling you . . ."

Holland interrupted, "Unless it's the truth, I'm not interested."

Annoyed by his tone, I shot back, "Will you let me speak?"

Holland countered, "All you're doing is saying 'This is the truth. This is the truth.' But it's not the 100 percent truth. It's not exactly what happened."

But it is 100 percent true! It's exactly what happened! Trying to back my way out of where the interview was going, I said, "I understand that I don't have a track record of truthfulness with you. But this happened the way I said it did. I don't care if you say it couldn't happen. That's what I did."

"Her arm can't fracture like that," he repeated.

"Let me say this: That is what I did at my house. If something happened some other place—that I don't have information about. I'm telling you what happened at my house. I gave her a hug and her arm popped."

In a tone that was a little too smug for my liking, Holland said, "I think you're correct. I think the break didn't happen at your house."

I don't have any idea what this guy is talking about. Confused,

I asked, "Where do you think it happened at? Do you think I did it at the tree festival?"

"I don't think it was malicious. You saying she sustained a spiral fracture because of a hug . . ." his tone was skeptical.

Having no desire to keep talking in circles, I finally asked, "What do you think I did? Be honest."

"I think your kids may have gotten away from you."

Now I'm even more confused. Seeking to clarify his position, I asked, "But what does that have to do with Abigail?"

Holland responded, "If you need to get after your kids so they didn't get hit by a car, hey, that may have happened."

Now I understood it loud and clear. *Oh my word. He thinks I broke Abigail's arm because I got mad when my kids ran away from me at the festival. He is making things up that didn't happen. He can't be serious. Who would come up with a theory like that?* I couldn't understand how Holland made the connection between Abigail's fracture and our earlier outing. If I was frustrated at the festival because my children ran off (which I wasn't), then I would have been more likely to break my own child's arm, not Abigail's. I also didn't understand how he came to believe that I broke Abigail's arm in a public space and nobody intervened or reported me. Nothing about his theory made sense.

When Holland divulged his theory, I should have stopped talking, calmly exited the interview room, and called an attorney. I should have realized that the investigation was turning out exactly how I feared it would—with an investigator not believing my story and then making up a cockamamie hypothesis about what I did that I absolutely did not do—and taken steps to protect myself. When someone with a gun and handcuffs who has the power to arrest you invents a scenario as irrational as Holland's, you should stop trying to reason with that person. I should have switched from reasoning mode to self-protection mode, but I didn't. I just kept forging ahead.

Trying to argue Holland out of his position, I said, "Don't you think someone would notice? Don't you think she would be like, 'Ow'? Don't you think she would have cried? She didn't cry when we were out. At home she was already upset, so that's why her arm popping didn't register as significant. I think you're off base."

Holland replied, "You're not going to hear a pop with a spiral fracture."

This news stopped me like nothing else in the interview had. Suddenly curious, I said "Oh, you don't? Then what was the pop?"

"I don't know."

"Are you sure?"

Falling back on his experience, he said, "Yeah, I've been doing it for a while."

This was a pivotal moment. The pop was what connected the hug to the break. But if spiral fractures don't produce a popping sound, then what if *I* was off base?

For the first time, I started to doubt myself. Thinking out loud, I said, "Well . . . then maybe I didn't break her arm at my house."

Sensing an opening, Holland explained, "It would be like your husband giving you a big hug or going to the chiropractor."

Slumped down a little in my chair, I put my fingertips to my temples and said, "Now I'm confused. Like, now I'm thinking it didn't happen when she was with me. Honestly."

I came into the interview convinced I caused the injury, but this new information planted a seed of doubt in my mind. Even while thinking on my feet in the middle of a stressful situation, I was beginning to doubt my guilt. Until this point, it had never occurred to me that I didn't cause Abigail's injury. From Meredith's initial phone call forward, I worked on the assumption that her injury occurred while she was in my care. I disregarded the necessary twisting to find a way that her injury happened while she was with me. I didn't understand until my second interview that if there was no twisting in anything that happened that day, then I couldn't be responsible for her broken arm.

Mentally I was in the middle of an awakening, but physically I was still in the interview with Holland, who was showing no signs of backing down. "I believe that you broke Abigail's arm," he said. "What I don't believe is how you said it happened."

Trying to come to terms with this new information while still actively participating in the interview, I replied, "The only thing I can say is what happened to the best of my knowledge. I hugged Abigail and something popped. Now I'm confused because I don't understand. I know there was a pop. At the time I thought it was her back. Maybe it *was* her back, because for the rest of the day she didn't act any different. All I can tell you is what I know."

Holland countered, "You're close but not all the way. I appreciate you saying you broke her arm. What I don't appreciate is that you're not being 100 percent truthful."

Still reeling, I said, "I *am* being 100 percent truthful. I guess what I'm saying now is that I *think* I broke her arm." Holland started to interrupt but I refused to let him. I continued, "Will you calm down and listen? Something popped, so I've been assuming that's when Abigail's arm broke. But now you're telling me it couldn't have happened that way."

Condescendingly, Holland said, "You say you broke it, then you say you didn't break it."

Exasperated by his inability to see my perspective, I said, "I didn't just say that! Don't put words in my mouth. I have believed that I broke her arm by giving her a hug and her arm being behind her back. Now you're telling me . . ." I trailed off, lost in my own rearranging thoughts.

Holland asked, "Why wouldn't you say anything at the beginning?"

Indignant, I replied, "Because of exactly what we're talking about right here! Exactly this. You're coming back at me with, 'I think you did it on Mass Street. I think you did it at Liberty Hall.' I didn't do *anything* on Mass. What you're doing right now is why I didn't say anything."

Holland asked a valid question, which was, "Why would anybody believe you?"

I responded, "I can't make people believe me. If you don't believe me, I can't control that. You're not going to get a different story out of me because there's nothing else I can say. Yes, I lied and left something out, but I can't make something up."

Holland responded, "Yeah you can. Anybody can."

"Why would I do that?"

"Because you don't want to get in trouble."

I attempted one more line of logic. "Holland, I'm already in trouble! You couldn't have done anything to me legally unless you had a confession, and I still came forward. You didn't call me. I called you. You didn't drag me down here."

Although we hadn't raised our voices, the exchange had grown heated in the last few minutes. And now Holland leveled an accusation: "And you still won't take a polygraph."

Having nothing to hide, I immediately replied, "Oh no, I'll take one. I'll absolutely take one. Today, tomorrow, next week, next month. I'll take one. Absolutely."

Unknowingly, I had just spoken the magic words necessary for Holland to even consider my innocence. He visibly softened and sat back in his chair like he was considering me in a new light. He said, "So you're maintaining that's the truth and you would even take a polygraph now."

"Give me a damn polygraph! Hook me up. Am I nervous? Yeah, but now I'm nervous because you don't believe me. If I pass, will you believe me?"

"If you pass it, I'll close the door."

And with that, our rapid-fire back-and-forth interview suddenly ended. Holland said he would call to schedule the polygraph, and with the understanding that the polygraph was my only chance, I collected my purse, walked out of the interview room, and went home.

Agreeing to take the polygraph was a no-brainer because I wasn't withholding anything anymore. I could answer all the questions without stress because I had already told everything about my day. I had nothing to worry about. I didn't need an attorney, because now that I had told my whole story, I was going to pass the polygraph. This was my one chance to prove to Daniel Holland that I had no other information to offer him besides the bear hug. In a perverse way, I actually looked forward to the polygraph because once it was over, I would be vindicated. More importantly, I would be done with the KBI.

❧

I walked out of the police station with a completely different perspective on what had happened on December 2, 2013. For weeks I writhed under the guilt of thinking I had broken Abigail's arm when I hugged her, but now? I doubted that I caused Abigail's injury at all. I went into the interview scared, distraught, and ready to relieve my tormented spirit. I left the interview asking, *What the hell just happened?*

Holland and I both learned new information during this interview. He learned that I believed the hug caused the spiral fracture, and I learned that a hug can't cause a spiral fracture. What we each did with that new information varied greatly. I took the information he gave, incorporated it into my experience, and let it lead me in a new direction. I figured that if spiral fractures don't pop and aren't caused by compression, then her injury might not have occurred when she was with me. I asked multiple questions about her injury so I could gather facts. I allowed those facts to change my opinion about what had happened, because it's okay to change your mind.

Across the table, Holland did the opposite. Instead of going where my information led him, he doubled down. He immediately dismissed the hug as a cover story without exploring it, because he had already decided that I broke her arm at the Festival of Trees. The hug was the truth, but it wasn't the truth that Holland had already decided on. Unless I repeated his version of events back to him, he would be convinced I was lying. He was correct, of course, that I didn't break Abigail's arm when I hugged her. When I confessed the hug, Holland could have chosen to believe me, which would have prompted several more productive questions. Later I was struck by how few questions he actually asked me. He did nothing to explore why I thought the hug broke her arm. He didn't explore anything at all. Instead, he just kept repeating one statement in various forms: "You're not being 100 percent honest."

Holland could have asked so many more questions: What was it about the hug that made you think it caused a fracture? Was it something about her demeanor, something about how hard you hugged her, or just a bad guess? Why did you think the popping sound meant her arm broke at that time? Has her back ever popped before? Why did you initially think going through the gate could have caused the injury? Describe another time on a different day when Abigail cried like she was crying on this day. How was that the same or different? When she cried on this day, what activities was she engaging in? When she wasn't crying, what activities was she engaging in?

And because he had already interviewed Steve and Meredith Holder, what Daniel Holland should have asked me to do but didn't—a line of questioning so painfully obvious it hurts—was this: "Start at the beginning of your day with Abigail and go over every behavior she engaged in, every reaction she had to every action you took, no matter how subtle, starting when Steve Holder opened your front door at 8:00 in the morning." Had he taken that approach, we could have figured some things out together.

⁓

I couldn't quite put my finger on it, but just like Meredith's initial phone call on December 2, something felt off when I left that second interview. Something was missing, but I couldn't figure out what. Since the very beginning of the investigation, I was so focused on the police and Child Protective Services that I wasn't watching out for anybody else. The things I was ready to defend myself against were incompetence, errors in judgment, and generalized stupidity. I wasn't prepared for the one thing that I would never be able to overcome: betrayal.

Chapter 5

The Predicament

THE FACT THAT the hug didn't cause Abigail's break was a relief because it meant that I wasn't a child abuser, but it added another layer of stress and confusion. If my hug didn't break Abigail's arm, then what did? I spent every day between my second interview and my polygraph rehashing the events of December 2, 2013. I started at the beginning of the day and played it all the way through trying to figure out what caused Abigail's injury. When I finished, I started back at the beginning and did it all again.

After days of running through every single action from that day, I finally had to reason with myself. If I had twisted Abigail's arm hard enough to break it, it would have been an event. I wouldn't have to go back through every part of my day to figure out when twisting might have occurred, because a twisting motion like that would have been notable. Everybody who has ever cared for young children knows the different cries they make. Abigail never cried out in pain as if she had just been injured. She cried and whined often enough, but there was never a time when her crying started directly after an event that would have resulted in a broken arm.

I finally stopped repeating the day when I realized that, in addition to not twisting Abigail's arm, I have never twisted the arm of any child I have ever provided care for, including my own children and the children I babysat as a teenager. Aggressively twisting the arm of a child is not my go-to response to things.

I'm not a perfect parent. Sometimes I'm a good mom, and sometimes I'm not. Sometimes I'm a good person, and sometimes I'm not. A solid 50 percent of my parenting involves overreacting and then apologizing for overreacting. I yell at my kids. Sometimes I regret yelling, and I'll apologize to the kids and explain why I yelled and what I should have done differently. Sometimes I don't regret yelling, and I tell them that too.

But grabbing a child and twisting their arm? That has never happened.

I haven't twisted much of anything since 2005, when I was diagnosed with rheumatoid arthritis, an autoimmune disease affecting the joints. Following a throat infection that didn't respond to antibiotics, every joint in my hands became stiff and swollen along with the joints in my hips, knees, ankles, and shoulders. The pain in my right wrist was so significant that I thought it was broken. When I finally saw a rheumatologist and she said, "You have rheumatoid arthritis," I burst into tears and explained, "I'm sorry I'm crying. I was hoping I would feel better soon."

My medical chart in the months before the active investigation paint a bleak picture: "Disease is very active. Patient cannot bring her fingers to her palms on her right hand. I am concerned she is going to sustain joint damage and lose function." Rheumatoid arthritis has always affected various joints throughout my body, but my hands and shoulders have always been the most bothersome. The pain is a constant ache incomparable to anything else I've felt. It makes even the simplest tasks challenging, and the stiffness makes routine movements difficult. A twisting motion has always been the most complicated motion for me because it involves grabbing an object, closing my fingers, and twisting at my wrist. Twisting is mechanically very simple, but for someone with rheumatoid arthritis, even grabbing a toy can be daunting.

At the time of the investigation, I often didn't have the strength in my hands to open a water bottle. Something so simple required assistance from Mike or Ryan. My shoulders were also an afflicted area. They routinely ached so much that if I wanted to lift my arm above my head to retrieve something up high, I would have to use one arm to push the other up at the elbow. My movements at this time would never have been described as violent, quick, or sudden. Rather, my actions were labored, deliberate, and painful.

My functioning wasn't the only concern. The inflammation resulted in fluid-filled knobs on my fingers that made my hands look awful. During my exams with my rheumatologist, she would sometimes look at my hands and, instead of speaking, simply let out a long, frustrated sigh.

In my first interview, I explained my rheumatoid arthritis and how it affected my functioning. I showed Holland how I would have to wrap my forearms around Abigail like a hug to even pick her up, because I didn't have enough strength in my hands to support the whole weight of her body.

Had I twisted Abigail's arm hard enough to break it, not only would she have had a physical reaction to it, but *I* would have had a physical reaction to it. If I couldn't open a water bottle or pick Abigail up with my hands, it's a safe bet that I also couldn't have grabbed her arm and twisted hard enough to break it.

∽

After my second interview, I went back to my phone conversation with Meredith on January 8, 2014, when I told her that I knew how Abigail's injury had been caused. She said that Abigail was a little grumpy in the evening and added that she only cried when someone touched her arm. The second part of that statement was key. When I put it together with my newfound awareness that a hug can't cause a spiral fracture, I started understanding Abigail's behaviors differently. In addition to going over every *action* I took throughout our day together, I started analyzing Abigail's *reaction* to the things we did. It was like an eye exam when the optometrist flips to a different lens and asks, "Is it clearer now? How about now?"

Until now, I had assumed the grumpy look on Abigail's face when Steve brought her inside was because she was tired. After my second interview, I looked back and recognized that the look on her face was less like fatigue and more like anger—as if something had just happened that upset her.

She wasn't crying when Steve walked in the door, but she cried when he passed her to me. She whined when I touched her arm to position her in down dog. She cried when I took hold of her arm to remove her shirt for fingerpainting. She cried when I rubbed her arm to wash it off after I had helped her fingerpaint.

She fell asleep in the van on the way to Lawrence, and she didn't usually fall asleep that early in the day. Crying on the way home from Lawrence wasn't out of the ordinary, but the fact that she screamed at me when I set her down in the car was very abnormal. Abigail wasn't prone to outbursts like that, and it was so out of character that I laughed at her.

Crying all the way up the stairs as I carried her was also something different. She usually quieted down once I picked her up, but that day she cried continuously on the van ride home, when being removed from the van, all the way up the stairs, through the gate, down the hallway, throughout the hug, and down the stairs, and didn't quiet down until we were standing in the garage waiting for the boys to come upstairs.

Abigail was also an eater, so the fact that she didn't eat on December 2 was notable. Her refusal of food throughout the day—both for breakfast and lunch—was so out of character that

I mentioned it to Meredith at pick-up. I remembered now that she ate applesauce for breakfast, but only when I fed it to her. She wouldn't pick up the toast on her own.

Abigail smiled at me when I leaned over the pack-and-play to get her up from her nap, but she cried as soon as I picked her up. She was happy until I touched her.

None of these details had seemed important in real time. As we went through the day, I knew nothing about Abigail's morning routine other than she woke up at 5:30 a.m. and, as Steve described, had "a case of the Mondays." We went about our day as we normally would and, when she was cranky, I thought it was because she was tired and possibly teething. It never crossed my mind that something was actually wrong with her. When a child is cranky, you do not immediately assume something significant has happened, especially if you don't have a reason to think otherwise. Abigail's behaviors were subtle, but now that I was looking for them, they were undeniable.

I knew I didn't twist Abigail's arm at any point in our day. I knew she arrived in a bad mood and cried or whined when I touched her. I knew that she didn't eat meals and was a little out of sorts. I knew all of those things separately but, at this time, I couldn't put them together. I was aware of all the moving parts, but I couldn't combine them. I look back on it now and think, *It isn't even that hard! How did I not see it?!* I was traumatized by what was happening to me and emotionally unable to put all the facts together to arrive at the most logical conclusion: Abigail Holder arrived at my house already injured. Someone else injured Abigail, not me. She was dropped off at my house with a spiral fracture in her arm, and the person who did it was sitting back silently while the police blamed me for it.

Who would want to believe that?

Chapter 6

The Polygraph

CHILD ABUSE REPORTS can be complicated. Children lack the verbal and reasoning skills of an adult, so investigators have to be careful and avoid leading questions. Additionally, statements made by children, even if they give details, can be met with suspicion because they are so young and potentially unreliable. Family dynamics add to the difficulty, because children are more apt to be swayed by adults both within their family and within the system. Safety is also a concern because social workers can be dealing with extremely unsavory characters. Drugs and mental illness—along with the instability they both create—are constants, as is the fact that a client rarely wants to have contact with the social worker. Child Protective Services is a service nobody wants.

Not every allegation assigned for investigation turns out to be true. Some do, of course, but other times the allegation is false. And then there is a middle area where the allegation is not abusive or a false report, but is still a bad decision. In social worker parlance, we call that middle place *inappropriate*. For example, slapping your teenage daughter in the face for cussing you out is not abusive, it's "inappropriate" (depending, of course, on the caseworker you get).

The investigator's job is to gather facts and make decisions about people's lives, but separating fact from fiction is complicated. Who do you believe, and who do you not believe? Why do you not believe them? Is somebody lying, or are they just minimizing? Maybe they are doing neither and are instead just telling you the truth as they see it. Does someone you interviewed have a reason to lie and, if they are lying, how is the lie relevant to the allegation? What steps can you take to determine if the allegation happened and, if it did happen, what steps can you take to make sure it doesn't happen again? Family dynamics like divorce-custody issues, substance abuse, mental illness, children with behavior issues, and dysfunctional family patterns make sifting through information incredibly complicated. Sometimes I got it right, and sometimes I didn't.

It is not uncommon for divorced parents to use the child welfare system to mediate their custody battles by making hotline reports about their ex. It was a phenomenon that happened often enough that we always had to consider it as a possibility. If divorced parents used the system too often, I would explain to each of them, "You can either learn to solve your problem on your own or I can solve it for you, and I guarantee you're not going to like the way I solve it."

I was assigned a sexual abuse case alleging that the mom's boyfriend was sexually abusing her child. The complicating factor for me was that the parents of the child had significant divorce-custody issues, and each had made repeated bogus calls to the hotline about the other. This history made it challenging to determine if this current report was true or if the report was made to gain leverage in the custody case.

The child denied being sexually abused in the interview. I went into it convinced that the long history of divorce-custody issues was to blame for the report, and the girl's lack of disclosure fed into my theory. After my interview of the child, however, the mom's boyfriend was arrested on an unrelated charge. While in jail, he asked a friend of his to go to his house and throw out some paperwork. Unfortunately for the boyfriend, his friend read the paperwork, which turned out to be a description, in his own words, of his sexual assault of his girlfriend's child. The allegation that I assumed was fabricated was in fact true. Had it not been for the boyfriend's arrest and his nosy friend, I would have continued to assume that the child had not been sexually abused, and she wouldn't have received the necessary mental health treatment that she needed and deserved.

Sexual abuse cases sound distressing, but I greatly preferred them to physical abuse reports. A skull fracture, for example, could happen any number of ways. Maybe it was the result of abuse, or maybe the child was accidentally dropped. Physical abuse reports contain a lot of gray area and are harder to figure out, but sexual abuse reports are much more straightforward. At the end of physical abuse reports, I would sometimes wonder, *How could anybody know what really happened here?*

⁊

On my way to the police station for the polygraph, I took the long way so I could talk to myself. *You can do this. This isn't too hard for you. You're going to be able to answer every question they ask because you're not lying anymore.* I was going into the polygraph with a clear understanding that I didn't twist Abigail's arm, but I was still very confused about how or when her injury occurred. This critical element I was missing—the *when*—was the biggest hurdle in my defense.

Sergeant Victor Lockhart (the officer who had responded to the initial abuse report and accompanied Holland to my house to execute the search warrant) met me in the lobby and led me back to the interview room. He was friendly and casual as we walked down the hallway. I told him, "I wish I had been honest in the very beginning."

He responded, "Hey, that's all right. You're getting it over with now."

As I entered the interview room, the agent who would be administering my polygraph—an enormous bear of a man named Scott Campbell—rose to meet me. He introduced himself and shook my hand. He was nice in the way that police officers are nice before they start being mean.

Before we even sat down, Campbell said, "It's resolved that you heard a pop and broke her arm."

Undeterred by him coming at me right out of the gate, I replied, "No, I *thought* that's what happened, but Holland said it couldn't be that. If spiral fractures don't pop and can't be caused by a hug, then I don't know what happened."

As we took our seats, Campbell explained that there would be two parts to the exam. We would begin with an interview portion where he would question me about events on December 2, 2013. Following that, I would be hooked up to a machine to monitor my stress response while I answered questions.

I thought that if I could explain all the things about Abigail's behaviors that I had come to understand since my second interview—including her demeanor when she entered my house—then perhaps the agents would understand that I never hurt her, even accidentally. My plan hit a roadblock right away, though, when Campbell said, "We aren't going to rehash the day when she was dropped off at 8:00 a.m. I don't care about that." He let me know straightaway the limitations he was placing on the interview.

Quickly referencing our morning before the outing, Campbell asked, "Was there any fussiness prior to the Festival of Trees?"

Seeing an opportunity, I explained, "Abigail wasn't in a great mood. When she came up the stairs I could tell she was in a funk, and her dad said she had a case of the Mondays. I told Meredith she had a 'holiday hangover.' There were certain things Abigail *didn't* do in the morning that was unusual. She didn't eat breakfast. She didn't fingerpaint. She didn't eat toast, but I fed her applesauce. She wasn't in a fantastic mood, but I also didn't think something was wrong with her."

Campbell didn't pay a bit of attention to the huge clues I had just given him. Instead, he said, "There are areas of concern where this could have happened. Holland is fixated on the Festival of Trees. There was passing through a gate. A hug. We are thinking if it happened, it happened during one of those times. I think the Festival of Trees is the most likely place because you had so many small children with you."

This again, but with a twist. The Festival of Trees theory still didn't make sense to me, but Campbell's explanation of why he believed it made it seem a little less like something coming out of left field. I understood how it looked to outsiders when I took so many little kids on outings of any kind. Taking care of small children intimidates some people, but not me. I always preferred an outing with kids to sitting at home. Sitting at home is boring. Going out is fun.

The majority of the interview was redundant, mainly because my story hadn't changed. Campbell asked me to narrate the Festival of Trees and the gate incident, and so for the third time I went over every detail I could remember. He asked me more detailed questions about the hug than Holland had. One question I thought was especially insightful was, "Did you feel the pop when you hugged her?"

"No, I didn't feel anything pop," I explained, not having considered this before he asked. "I just heard it."

In addition to more detailed questions, Campbell asked me to do something that I thought was clever and helpful: He handed me a doll and told me to demonstrate how I hugged Abigail. I stood up, clutched the doll to my chest, bent over at the waist like I was lying it on a bed, and hugged the doll.

During my detailed recounting of our day, I denied that any

twisting motion occurred at any time. After we had exhausted every detail, Campbell said, "Well, people minimize," insinuating that something more significant had happened than what I let on.

Campbell and Holland had me in a tough spot. I wasn't lying or minimizing when I described the hug. To use Holland's phrase, I was telling the 100 percent truth. Unfortunately, the only way Scott Campbell and Daniel Holland would believe me was if I said that I violently twisted Abigail's arm. Ironically, in order for them to believe I was telling the truth, I would have had to lie.

As we wound down the interview portion of the exam, Campbell explained, "I'm not interested in a criminal case against you, but I think you caused this injury."

Expecting as much, I said, "Oh, so you think it was me?" And then, because I was aware of my limited defenses, I restated, "All I can tell you is what happened."

I didn't have access to all the information that had been gathered up to this point, and I still wasn't sure when her injury occurred. When Scott Campbell indicated he believed the injury occurred in my care, I had to accept that he was privy to information that I didn't have. Even knowing this, I still didn't budge. I said what I had already said and would continue to say: *All I can tell you is what happened.*

After the initial interview, we moved to the actual polygraph exam. Prior to being hooked up to the polygraph wires, Campbell explained the process and the three questions I would be asked:

1. Did you twist Abigail's arm?
2. Did you injure Abigail's arm by twisting it?
3. Was Abigail's arm injured before you gave her the bear hug?

The third question confused me. My honest answer to this question was, "I don't know," but only yes or no was acceptable.

Campbell clarified that I had previously indicated there was nothing that took place before the bear hug that would have injured her arm. With this clarification, I understood that the question's purpose was to establish if I did anything before the hug that would have injured her arm, not necessarily whether her arm was broken before the hug or not. The answer to that question is no, so that's how I answered.

I was also given what Scott Campbell referred to as "directed lie" questions that were intermingled with the three questions specific to Abigail during the polygraph.

The questions were:

1. Have you ever said anything in anger that you later regretted?
2. Did you ever tell a lie to someone who trusted you?
3. Did you ever make a mistake?

In explaining the directed lie questions, Campbell instructed me to think of specific scenarios where I had done what they were asking me about. However, when I was asked about them during the polygraph, I was instructed to lie and say I had never done it. When Campbell asked if I've ever made a mistake, I was to think about that one time I drove forty-five miles per hour through a construction zone and got pulled over—and I was supposed to lie and say no. Lying was supposed to spike my anxiety to give the agents a comparison for the Abigail-specific questions.

Campbell explained that a polygraph has two possible outcomes: pass or fail. He stated, "You pass if you tell the truth and fail if you lie." I was telling the truth, so I fully expected to pass. As Campbell placed the blood pressure monitor on my finger, I apologized for how my hands looked—swollen and knobby—and explained that I have rheumatoid arthritis. He didn't comment on this. As we were preparing for the exam, in a casual tone almost like he had forgotten something, Campbell handed me a piece of notebook paper and instructed me to write the number five in the middle of it. I was then instructed to lie and say that I didn't write the number five in the middle of the paper that I was holding. He stated that this would give him a baseline to gauge when I was truthful and when I was lying. I thought this bizarre, but I didn't tell Campbell that.

The polygraph exam itself was relatively simple. The questions about Abigail were mixed in with the directed lie questions. Campbell asked me each question several times, and I would answer. I was relatively calm throughout, but whenever he would get to a question about Abigail, I could feel my stomach churn and my heart rate increase like I was going down the initial drop on a roller coaster. I swung back and forth from calm to nervous throughout the exam.

When the polygraph exam was over, I thought I had done a decent job, all things considered. That's why I was floored when Scott Campbell indicated that I failed. (Later I would hire a criminal attorney who was a former prosecutor. He gave me a helpful tidbit of information I wish I had known before the exam: The KBI tells you that you failed a polygraph whether you did or not to "scream at you and get you to confess.")

Campbell said, "There's something you haven't come clean about."

I replied, "I don't know of any twisting. I know you think I do but I don't."

"The question 'Did something happen before the hug?' had the second highest rate."

Trying to dampen my frustration, I said, "This is sad, because I actually think I did a good job. When you would say *Abigail* my stomach would roll."

Campbell rejoined, "I'm aware of that when it's someone's own child. I don't think you broke her arm maliciously. I think it was frustration."

I repeated what I'd already told them both so many times: "I don't think I twisted her arm in anger or frustration. I don't think I twisted her at all. I think *you guys* think that."

Slightly indignant, Campbell quipped, "I do now."

Why is this happening? "This is ridiculous," I exclaimed, "I don't know what to say. All I can say is what happened. I don't know how this injury was caused. I thought I did it when I gave her a hug. But that's not it. Then Holland started talking about downtown on Mass Street. Yes, she fell, but I didn't yank or twist her."

"Earlier you said she stumbled." I was instantly annoyed that Scott Campbell chose to believe that using the words *fell* and *stumbled* was somehow a discrepancy. Out of everything he could have focused on, he chose to focus on semantics.

I explained, "I was holding her with my right hand and she fell." If I was using my right hand to hold Abigail's hand, I would have been holding her left hand. But her right arm was the one with the spiral fracture.

"Did she cry?"

"No." I was starting to become overwhelmed. "Holland said if I passed then I would be done and now I'm not going to be done. I don't know what to say."

Campbell said, "I don't believe you snapped, but I do believe this injury occurred because you were frustrated. There's something else here that you're not telling."

My frustration was mounting. "You've given me a million outs. If there was something else to say I would say it. I don't know what else to say."

Campbell helpfully turned the computer monitor towards me so that I could see the graph that was generated during my exam showing my stress response. It showed a line like a heart monitor and I could see several instances when the graph spiked.

I asked, "Do the numbers go up every time there is a question about her?"

"Yes, every time."

I said, "Oh, absolutely. Absolutely. Every time you say her name my stomach rolls."

"That's why we put the directed lie questions in so you're getting the same feeling."

"But that's not the same. Answering a question about a made-up lie is not the same as answering a question about Abigail. The thing about Abigail actually means something. No, I didn't twist her arm. No, I didn't injure her."

Campbell indicated I was exposed to the questions about Abigail fourteen times during the exam. I said, "Yeah, it's kind of a big deal for me. Holland said if I pass this I'm done. I don't have any other info to put forward. Now you guys are going to think I did something intentional. *I don't know what happened.*"

He countered, "I don't think it was intentional."

"I didn't even do anything accidentally."

"I think you feel trapped because you've given this account."

"This is a nightmare! I really thought the hug was what caused the break. When you hear a pop and you think back . . . Wouldn't I have come up with something better than that?"

"I think you came up with the hug account . . ."

I interrupted and said, "No, the hug happened."

Campbell continued, "I think in your mind it's showing that the injury occurred during an affectionate moment."

"This is insane. You have to be making this up." Pointing to the monitor I said, "I think I passed that and you're trying to get me to say something else. This is exactly what I thought was going to happen, that you guys were going to do this. *Nothing else happened.* If you say you think it happened when I had care of her, okay, but if it did, then I don't know when."

Feeling frustrated with Campbell and the polygraph results, I made a request that, in hindsight, is almost comical in its naivety: I requested to speak to the individual who didn't believe anything

I said and who had already proven himself illogical. I asked, "Can I talk to Daniel Holland, please?"

When Holland entered the room, I said, "I know you're going to come in here and say I did it by accident. *I don't know.*"

Like a recording, Holland asked, "Why were you not 100 percent honest?"

"When I didn't tell you about the bear hug at first? Because I was afraid you guys would think it was malicious or mean."

Holland asked, "Why did you hug her?"

"Because she's cute." *Why else do you hug a child?*

He asked me to describe the hug again. I did so as I had done twice before and then I said, "It's always the same story."

Up until this point, Holland had been adamant that the hug didn't cause the injury. Now he had switched gears and was asking about the hug as if it were important. After describing it for him again, I said, "Now you think there's something in the room. It's always going to be the same story. I didn't twist her arm. I wasn't mad at her that day. I wasn't mad that day at all. I'm going to keep giving you the same answers."

He moved briefly to my previous employment, "You used to work at DCF and would have received training on spiral fractures." Although I probably did receive training on spiral fractures at some point in my career, I have no recollection of it specifically. If I worked a physical abuse report and I needed to know how a specific injury occurred, I would call the doctor or police officer and ask how the injury was likely to have happened. I had no need to carry that information around inside my own brain.

Holland changed tactics. Instead of repeating that I needed to tell the truth and occasionally throwing in a question, he went on the attack. He began, "I don't know what's more despicable—that you hurt a kid or that you're choosing to lie about it."

I didn't look at Holland as he spoke. I alternately stared into space or at my lap, and then I calmly repeated myself once again:

"I did not twist her arm. I did not yank her. I did not pull her. I did not intentionally harm her. I don't know what to say."

Holland still wasn't finished. "Your friends and husband know you're a liar."

"I've had a million outs. Why not just take one? I don't know what to say."

He pressed on, "At least say you're sorry. At least offer her that. You won't take ownership for it."

"How can I take ownership for something I don't even know I did? I can't say something I didn't do. There was no twisting, yanking, pulling that I'm aware of."

"So when I have my conversation with Meredith, that's what I can tell her? That I asked Andrea if she was sorry and she wasn't even sorry?"

I am done with this man. I shot back, "Spoken like a typical cop. If you choose to give her that line of bullshit then you go ahead and do that. That's not what I said and you know it."

I should have kept my mouth shut. I wish I hadn't let Holland provoke me. I should have elevated myself, and I did the opposite. I had just back-sassed a police officer in front of his co-worker, and that's never a good idea.

Holland's jaw clenched. "Are you sorry you broke her arm or not?"

"I don't know that I did."

He asked, "You're not going to fail a polygraph if you're telling the truth, correct?"

"Obviously I'm telling the truth and I failed a polygraph, so there's your answer."

Holland and I were at an impasse. He was going to keep saying I did it, and I was going to keep saying I didn't. When Holland started spiraling downward, I decided that I had had as much of him and Scott Campbell as I was willing to take and I got up to leave.

As I stood there preparing to exit the room with my purse on my shoulder, I asked, "What are the next steps?"

"Sit back down," he ordered.

I stood anchored in the doorway, making no move to follow his directive.

He said, "You're heartless."

"You're not going to goad me into saying anything else, Daniel."

Holland wouldn't give me any information on what was going to happen next unless I took my seat, and so I left the interview room, walked down the hallway, out the front door and got into my car. Finally alone without Holland or Campbell badgering me, I took a moment to breathe, backed out of the parking lot, and drove home.

⤳

I place zero importance on my polygraph results. The machine showed that I was anxious when Campbell questioned me about Abigail, and why wouldn't I have anxiety about that? The baselines Campbell established weren't authentic to how my mind and body process lying. I didn't care at all whether he thought I lied about writing the number five on a piece of paper. I cared *a lot* about him thinking I broke Abigail's arm. The directed lie questions didn't carry any personal weight for me, so they didn't trigger any anxiety response. Using directed lie questions as a comparison to felony child abuse is like trying to measure how anxious somebody gets around snakes by showing them a kitten.

In my ten years working for CPS, I had the pleasure of working with various highly skilled, highly effective detectives. I can't remember one time when one of those detectives gave a suspect a polygraph test. Rather, they thoroughly interviewed all relevant parties, followed all leads, and relied on interviewing skills to determine what occurred and resolve the case. A polygraph is no substitute for interviewing skills and simple smarts, and Daniel Holland exhibited neither. He asked minimal questions and made assumptions with no facts to back them up, and then relied on the polygraph exam to prove his theory.

The lead detective doesn't administer the polygraph. They just pass the information along to the examiner. The examiner is supposed to be objective—but Holland had briefed Campbell on everything that he thought about the case. It's hard to believe that the information gathered from the lead detective wouldn't sway the examiner at least a little bit. And what if the information given to the polygraph examiner by the lead detective is wrong? What if the lead investigator is incompetent? What if he missed key facts? What if he didn't ask the right questions during their interviews? What if he forgot to mention something to the polygraph examiner that was of critical importance? What if he targeted the wrong person?

Chapter 7

The Light Bulb Moment

I WAS COMPLETELY overwhelmed by the time I drove back home. The fact that I couldn't seem to make anybody believe what I was saying was beyond frustrating. I needed some sort of mediator to explain to them what I was saying, because when I spoke, they didn't understand. I was initially resistant to hiring an attorney, but now I had no other option.

Mike and I chose a firm staffed by former prosecuting attorneys who now operated on the opposite side of the law. At our initial meeting, I informed them that, because of the conflict of interest involving Mike's profession, the investigating agency was the KBI. One attorney asked me who the assigned KBI agent was. At the same time I said, "His name is Daniel Holland," the attorney said, "Please tell me it's not Daniel Holland."

I gave the attorneys a rundown of what had transpired in the case, including my initial lie, my decision to tell the truth, meeting with Holland for a second interview, Holland's theory on the Festival of Trees, and my polygraph test that I was told I failed. One of the attorneys would contact the assigned lawyer in the attorney general's office to ask that a meeting take place prior to a charging decision being made. Outside of that, we would simply wait to see what happened next. I was instructed not to speak with anyone about my case.

In the days after my polygraph interview but before meeting with the lawyers, I continued going over the day I spent with Abigail. I knew I remembered her behavior correctly—namely, that she cried or whined when I touched her—but one thing threw me for a loop: the bongo drums. My video of Abigail playing the bongo drums showed a seemingly happy, content, uninjured child. Her right arm showed no signs of bruising or swelling, and her countenance was untroubled. She seemed pleased with herself. Even though I knew her odd behaviors started right when she walked into my house, I couldn't reconcile how she would be able to play the bongo drums with a broken arm.

I went back to what Meredith said about Abigail's behavior at their residence that night: Abigail only cried when a member of her family touched her arm. I wasn't touching Abigail's arm when she played the bongo drums. I also wasn't touching Abigail's arm when we walked around the Festival of Trees and on Massachusetts Street, the other time during our day when she was at her happiest. The bongo drums and our outing had something else in common: they were both things that Abigail enjoyed and was most distracted by. Music time was her favorite activity inside our house, and strolling down Massachusetts Street was her favorite activity outside our house.

I also considered Abigail's pain tolerance, which is something I shared with Daniel Holland in my first interview. Whenever she would fall, instead of crying, Abigail would act like she meant to fall. If she fell in the grass, she would gently feel the grass to make everybody believe she meant to fall to be closer to the ground. It was a running joke between her parents and me. When she would fall, I would often wonder if this was the time when she would cry, but she never did. Abigail was one tough cookie.

Besides Abigail's behaviors, there were other things, too—things that had no meaning when they occurred but suddenly had tremendous significance as I put the pieces together.

When Meredith called me en route to the emergency room on December 2, 2013, she said, "Nothing happened at our house, because Steve was only alone with her for forty-five minutes." Only after the polygraph did I realize how odd that statement was, like maybe she would have believed that Steve could have hurt Abigail, except that he wasn't alone with her long enough to have done anything.

I had sent Steve a text at 8:35 a.m. on December 2, 2013, asking, *Did Abigail eat breakfast already or is she just on a hunger strike?* Steve responded twenty-two minutes later, *She hasn't eaten yet this morning. Maybe a couple of bites of her sister's meal this morning. Not sure what her deal could be.* The quickness of Steve's return text surprised me because he usually wouldn't respond to my texts at all. I had stopped sending him pictures as often as I did Meredith because I assumed he was too busy at work. As I sifted through these memories and information, I thought that it was possible that Steve just had more time that morning, or maybe he responded because I had asked him a direct question. But now, I wondered if he replied so quickly because he was nervous about Abigail's behavior.

When I told Steve that I had to take a polygraph, he initially had a startled look on his face with wide eyes and a blank stare before he composed himself. I initially interpreted that look as concern for me, which it could have been. But what if his expression was actually concern for himself? If I had to take a polygraph, maybe Steve was worried he'd have to take one too.

Back in November of 2013, Meredith began asking me if she could bring Abigail over to my house at 6:00 a.m. when she went to work so that Steve "wouldn't be rushing her around in the morning." At the time, I hedged because I didn't want to be watching Abigail at 6:00 a.m. while the rest of the Holder family was home asleep.

Meredith had also told me that Steve didn't like it when she kept changing her schedule around to include working early mornings.

I once heard a Holder family member laugh about how angry Steve would get in the morning. When I heard this, I wasn't concerned, because morning routines are notoriously stressful in families with school-aged kids. You can likely find morning anger in a lot of households in America at some point during the school year.

Meredith never even seemed upset with me when Abigail's arm was broken. She never thought that I was the one who hurt Abigail, even though I was the only logical suspect outside of her family. What if Meredith knew—or suspected—who hurt Abigail? What if she was letting me take the fall for something she knew I didn't do?

On the way home after meeting with the attorneys, I finally told Mike everything that had been brewing in my mind: "I think Abigail's arm was broken before she was dropped off, and I think Steve did it." And one by one, I described all the pieces I had been sorting through. I saw the realization slowly settle into Mike's face. At first his expression was one of attentive listening, but as I went through my list his facial expression moved to one of *knowing*. Suddenly everything made sense.

Once I said it out loud to Mike, I couldn't stop saying it out loud. I wrote an email to my attorneys indicating that I thought Steve broke her arm in the morning. I told my therapist, my friends, my mom. Everyone was supportive and understanding; one friend went so far as to acknowledge that she would have behaved the same way had she been in my position. I still felt like I had been hit by a truck.

I didn't know why I couldn't say it until we were in the car on the ride home. I didn't know why I couldn't make myself say the words to my attorneys, or even to Mike before now. Why couldn't I stand up for myself? I didn't want to acknowledge what had happened to me because that betrayal was too hard and painful to accept. Saying the words, "I think Steve broke Abigail's arm before he dropped her off, and he hasn't said anything while I've gotten in trouble" would make them true—and I didn't want them to be true. Why would I ever want to believe that someone I trusted would do that to me?

⤚

I understand why the hug scenario sounds so weird and illogical to investigators. It *is* weird and illogical. It doesn't make sense for me to think a hug caused a spiral fracture, so why did I believe it? In hindsight, the only reason I thought I caused Abigail's injury was that Meredith said I did.

When Meredith first called me on the way to the hospital in December, I made two assumptions. First, I believed Meredith when she said she didn't think Abigail's arm was injured by someone in her family. I also assumed that nobody in the Holder family would hurt Abigail and let the police blame me for it. I was wrong on both counts.

In December, my mother, my father-in-law, and my friends indicated they believed someone in Abigail's family was responsible for her injury but wasn't speaking up about it. I didn't believe that to be true and neither did Mike. Before I told Mike about the hug, he assumed that Abigail's injury was caused at her own house, and he said so to Daniel Holland in his interview. But if anyone suggested that someone in the Holder family was hanging me out to dry, Mike would respond in the same way that I did: *They wouldn't do that. It's not like that. They're good people.* We weren't on guard against the Holder family. As far as I could see, the only force working against me was the police, but while

I focused on the cops, the person responsible for Abigail's broken arm was wreaking havoc with their silence.

Steve and Meredith Holder were two of the last people I would have believed could have betrayed me. They had never given me any indication that they were anything other than what they appeared: kind, friendly, and of good character.

The Holders were not strangers to me. In fact, we had weaved in and out of each other's lives in a way that now seems nearly destined. My oldest son, Ryan, and Steve's oldest son, Jared, were born in the same hospital hours apart. A few short years later Ryan and Jared went to the same preschool. Their classrooms were close by, but they never met each other. Meredith—who would later become Jared's stepmother—was Ryan's preschool teacher before she and Steve ever met or started dating.

At the time, I was a single mother, and Ryan and I moved seven miles from Lawrence, Kansas, to Eudora in July 2005. Steve also made the move at some point, which is when Ryan and Jared found each other and latched on tight. Years later, in a piling on of cosmic connection, Meredith arrived as Steve's girlfriend at an end-of-the-year parent-child scrimmage in middle school. Our paths had been orbiting for years, but always for good. I never envisioned that they would collide in such a devastating way.

I had already determined that the Holder family posed no threat to me, so when Meredith indicated I was responsible for the injury, I believed her. She and Steve had never given me any reason not to. I never believed—and still have a hard time believing—that Steve would be capable of dropping off his injured child at my house, not give me any information about why she might be upset, and then leave her with me the entire day without mentioning anything.

My initial response might have been different if I had thought even for a moment that the Holders were deceptive. Instead, the one thing keeping me from putting the puzzle pieces together was that I couldn't comprehend that they would sell me out like that. I wouldn't have done that to them—and didn't, because I called Holland right when I learned he was turning his attention to the Holders. I assumed that meant the Holders wouldn't do that to me. More than that, I didn't think *anybody* would do this to me. When you live your life a certain way, you believe you're immune to entanglement with the system. Getting hoodwinked by your friends and waylaid by the cops is something that happens to "other people." I never thought something like this would happen to somebody like me.

After I figured out that Steve most likely had something to do with Abigail's arm, the next logical step should have been to call the lead investigator on the case and share my realization. Unfortunately, the lead investigator on my case was Daniel Holland. It's a hard thing when the person you should trust the most is a person you can't trust at all.

Chapter 8

The Perspective

SOME OF US think about child abuse in stereotypes: a greasy-haired man with no job prospects and zero ambition, who spends the majority of his time sitting in a plastic lawn chair in his back yard wearing a white ribbed tank top and drinking Natty Light beer at two in the afternoon while Guns N' Roses plays on the transistor radio. Sometimes child abusers look *exactly* like that, but my experience working for the State showed a wide variety of clients. Anyone can be reported for child abuse or neglect—most of them poor, some middle-class or even wealthy, some smart, some who function at a lower level, some who are trying their best with the hand they've been dealt, and others who struggle each and every day.

I've met people with highly successful, seemingly problem-free lives who think they arrived there under their own prowess. For the most part, I believe your choices are the primary force in your life, but I also understand that others' choices can be just as powerful as your own. Life is easy when you encounter only green lights, but if you had experienced some of the abuse that my clients did, you might have grown up to be a drug addict too.

In instances of generational abuse or neglect, I often wonder at what point we stop feeling sorry for someone. How big of a mess do you have to make of your children's lives before we stop caring how messy your own childhood was? When does your own child abuse stop counting?

Certain people have life trajectories like this: grow up in a two-parent household; attend a private high school; graduate from the college of your choice with no student loans because your parents paid your way; start working at the job your dad got for you; get married in a lavish ceremony followed by a honeymoon on the beach; buy a $500,000 house; have three kids; retire and spoil your grandkids.

Others' lives look like this: grow up with a single parent and use food stamps to pay for your groceries; move once a year to a different apartment or trailer; get molested by your mom's boyfriend; watch your mom get beat up by her next boyfriend; spend time in foster care because your mom can't get it together; barely graduate high school because learning is not directly linked to your survival; become addicted to drugs to cope with the pain; have three kids by three different guys who are all clones of your mom's boyfriends because it's what you think you deserve; get clean; realize you got clean too late because your own children are repeating your life cycle; "retire" from your fast food job when you qualify for disability; watch your grandkids rotate on and off welfare and in and out of jail.

Most of my clients came from the second group. Getting ahead is hard when you don't even know what getting ahead looks like, and you don't know anybody who can show you. Being a good parent is challenging when you never had one yourself. My clients' lives were often raw and open because pretense has little room in a trailer park. I spoke to a college class once, and a student referenced the movie *Homeless to Harvard: The Liz Murray Story*. She asked if I witnessed stories like that very often in my job—stories about people overcoming insurmountable odds and achieving seemingly impossible feats. My answer was simple: "No. That's why it's a movie."

❧

Surprisingly, Steve has been the easiest person for me to forgive, even though I think he most likely injured Abigail. Steve wasn't unique—he wasn't the first person I had encountered who had injured his child. Working in child welfare, I learned to view people in the context of their lives, not just one choice they made.

I was assigned a report about a weeks-old infant who had bruising on his body. The parents were both in their early twenties, and the father, who had a history of criminal behavior, was also reported to be abusive to the mother. I arranged for the infant to be seen by a doctor, and x-rays showed that the child also had rib fractures. I applied for foster care because the father was a safety risk to the infant and the mother couldn't protect the child from harm. A short while later, I was assigned another report involving the same man but a different woman. She was pregnant and he was physically abusive to her. Not wanting to put this new baby in the same position as his older half-sibling, I removed the baby from the hospital when he was born, because the father had made no attempt to change his abusive behavior. He was likely to be just as dangerous to this newest baby and its mother.

Another time, an infant presented at the hospital with a skull fracture. This child resided with his parents, who were in their early- to mid-twenties. At Children's Mercy Hospital, the father gave an initial explanation for the injury that the assigned physician said did not fit the child's injury. The detective informed the father of this discrepancy, and the father cried and began describing what had happened. He had been working late and waking up early to care for his son. He was exhausted. As he was holding the child, he dropped a plate as he tried to put it in the drying rack. This angered him, and he reacted by aggressively throwing his infant son on the couch. He bounced off the couch and hit the floor, fracturing his skull. The father was devastated when he described these events. It was hard to watch. After his confession, he asked the officer to tell his wife what he had done. I don't think the man was afraid to tell the police what had happened. The person he was most afraid of telling was his wife. The police can send you to prison for nonfatal child abuse, but eventually you're released. If your wife turns on you, though, that's a prison that is much harder to leave.

For the first father, domestic violence—towards both women and children—was not an isolated event. It was a way of life. If left to his own devices, and without outside intervention, he could have (and probably would have) inflicted devastating injuries to any member of his family. His history of criminality, combined with injuries to girlfriends and one of his children, resulted in a man who was not safe. That didn't ring true for the second father. He inflicted the same injury on a child—a fracture—but his personal profile was vastly different. His violence was isolated, and he had no criminal history. He showed great and genuine remorse for his actions. As it played out, he ended up being a more appropriate parent for his children than his wife because, outside of this one event, he was more stable.

We can't lump everybody who hurts a child into the same category of Terrible Parent. Some caregivers absolutely need a punishment from the court system to change their behavior, because they're not motivated to change on their own. Other perpetrators of isolated child abuse don't need a jail cell to make them feel bad about their choices, because it's not possible for them to feel any worse than they already do. Some abuse is an isolated act in an otherwise nonviolent life, and these caregivers would likely make necessary changes even without outside intervention.

When several mothers I interviewed were confronted with

factual evidence of their child's father having broken the child's bones (such as the father admitting he did so), it was not uncommon for them to say, "But he didn't do it on purpose." It sounds like denial, but I understood what they were getting at. I don't think all the people who snap and shake or break their child do it on purpose. I don't think abuse is always a conscious decision—and I don't think it's an accident, either. I think it falls in the category invented by young children that is "accidentally on purpose."

During an investigation of a different man alleged to have caused a head injury to his child, I interviewed his family members, doctors, and friends. I was able to recognize that, outside of this incident, the dad was a fantastic parent. He was generally calm, mild-mannered, and involved in parenting his kids.

I told my co-worker, "This guy is a better parent than me."

Skeptical, she replied, "Andrea, he beat up his kid."

"Yeah, I know. But outside of that he's still a way better parent than me."

I meant what I said. He was probably a calmer, more attentive, and all-around better caretaker than I am. He just lost his mind in a more serious way than I ever have. His situation reinforces the reality that child abusers don't always look like monsters. Working at DCF helped me have less judgment towards the actions of others because I came to know that we are all capable of the things we assume we'll never do. We look at some people and say, "She's not the type to abuse her child." We look at others and say, "I'm not surprised he abused his child. He looks like the type." In my years as a social worker, I learned there is no type.

One of my favorite clients called me one afternoon and said, "Andrea, if you don't get over to my house right now, I'm gonna beat my kid's ass."

I replied, "Thanks for calling me before you did that. I'll be right over."

Her words might seem out of control to some, but she was in perfect control. She exemplified exactly what I wanted in a client, a caretaker of my children, and myself: she was at the breaking point and she knew it, so she called a trusted source, admitted her weakness, and asked for help. I didn't put her child in foster care. I didn't call her names or tell her she was a bad parent. I went over to her house, we all sat down and talked it through until everybody felt better, and I left. She and her children were safe.

The people who don't admit their parental freak-outs are in the greatest danger of high-diving into the deep end. When people won't admit they have almost lost it on a kid, I assume they're lying.

Perfect parenting doesn't exist, and, while not everybody breaks their child's bone, nobody should be out there thinking they are Parent of the Year. We are all flawed.

❧

Maybe Abigail's spiral fracture was abusive, or maybe it was an accident. If Steve lost his temper and twisted Abigail's arm, that didn't make him a bad person in my eyes. I had no desire to belittle or shame him, and one bad choice didn't cancel out the wealth of good parenting he had already demonstrated. With the limited information I had (and a fair amount of speculation), I figured Steve most likely had a bad morning and made a mistake. I've never broken a child's arm, but I've made plenty of mistakes.

The breaking of Abigail's arm is the one thing in this God-forsaken mess that I actually understand. I start to lose my way when Steve dropped her off at my house and let everybody think I caused her injury. He handed Abigail to me like a hot potato, told me nothing about her injury, gave me no information when I texted him about Abigail not eating breakfast, allowed me to go through an entire day with her, and then let investigators think that I broke her arm. That is a truth much harder to accept.

I've never thought Steve knew Abigail's arm was broken when he dropped her off, but he for sure knew once Meredith called him from the emergency room. He's smart enough to put two and two together. As each day passed, Steve became not only the person who knew how Abigail's arm was broken, but also the primary person who let me take the blame for it.

Steve had many opportunities to come to my defense. When he brought Abigail over in the morning, he could have explained why she was grumpy. When I sent him the text about breakfast, he could have told me that she wasn't eating because she might be in pain. When Meredith called to tell him that Abigail's arm was broken, he could have admitted what happened. When it was obvious the police were targeting me for something he knew I didn't do, he could have spoken up. When Mike told him the police took my phone, he could have recognized that things were serious and exonerated me. When I called Meredith to say I was going to confess to breaking Abigail's arm, he could have said, "No, she didn't. I did."

I would often have compassionate feelings towards Steve, and that gave me some peace. Then the anger would return when I remembered that he allowed me to call Daniel Holland and confess to something he knew I didn't do. I became resentful and judgmental, and I hated that, even though it was justified. I would hold on to these dark feelings until I could give them up. I would start to feel compassion again, but then I would remember that Steve said nothing when he knew Holland had confiscated my phone. Round and round I ran on the hamster wheel of forgiveness. I didn't want to be mad at Steve, but I couldn't stop. My shared history with the Holders complicated everything, and my feelings didn't know where to settle.

I also experienced a sense of nostalgic loss. I wanted to go back to the way it was before, when we would watch our kids play sports and cheer them on, commiserate over their behavior, or laugh at the dumb stuff they did. I didn't want to have lost what was gone, but none of us could go back. The only way forward was to let it go.

Interacting with Steve was actually much easier for me than seeing Meredith. I didn't seek him out, but if we ran into each other, I could acknowledge him while I could barely even look at Meredith. In addition to my empathetic understanding of his actions, there was another reason for this: Steve was the only other person on this planet (besides a preverbal child) who knew I was innocent. The last time I interacted with Meredith, I told her that I believed I caused the injury. I didn't know what she believed about my guilt or innocence, or what Steve had and hadn't told her, so when I saw her, I burned with words I wasn't able to say.

Steve probably stayed quiet because he was afraid of the consequences. Who wouldn't be? I know I was. Had he confessed, his consequences would be the same things I was up against. He would be arrested and booked into jail, where he would pose for a mugshot that would most likely be plastered on the front page of the local newspaper. Within the court system, he would have to either take a chance in a jury trial, where he would explain his side of events in the hopes of an acquittal (and risk a thirty-six-month prison sentence), or take a plea that would hopefully result in probation. And those are just his legal consequences. His personal consequences could be much more impactful.

I now have personal experience with how it feels to not want to get in trouble for hurting a child, and it would be hypocritical of me not to empathize with where he's coming from. I understand how he would be afraid of the reaction of his family, how it would affect the status of his kids with his ex-wife, how it would affect his job. Steve prioritized his own life ahead of mine and operated in a way that he felt protected what was his. It just happened that as he acted to protect himself and his family, he dropped a bomb on mine. That was hurtful, but maybe if I had lived the same life he lived up until that point I would have made the same choices.

Some people close to me think Steve has no guilt or regret over what he did to my life, but I don't think that's true. I believe if he could find a way to take it all back, he would do so in a heartbeat. I think, more than anything, it was simply convenient for Steve that he was scheduled to drop Abigail off with me at 8:00 a.m. If he could manage to get her to my house and leave her there all day, then of course everybody was going to think I injured her. I don't think he planned it out in advance, but he took full advantage of the opportunity. He also had quite a bit of help from the Eudora Police Department and the KBI. Daniel Holland and Victor Lockhart offered Steve a beautifully wrapped gift. All he did was reach out and take it.

It took me a while, but eventually I made complete peace in my heart with Steve. I don't have the energy or the desire to wish harm upon him in retaliation for what happened. In the end, this book isn't about Steve Holder and what he did or didn't do. It's about the people who let him get away with it.

Chapter 9

The Breakdown

AS AN ADULT, I have always been confident, but starting in January 2014 I felt timid and weak and afraid. The active investigation had already gone on for six weeks—and had included two interviews with Daniel Holland, a search warrant, a polygraph, and the realization that Steve had caused the injury—and I was exhausted. Being targeted by the police is not a common occurrence for me. I didn't have a wealth of personal experience to draw on to reorient myself. I couldn't call up a friend and say, "What did you do when this happened to you?" because this had never happened to anybody I knew. I didn't know the protocol. What is the next step after you've been accused by the police of something you didn't do? What do you do when you tell the police that you are innocent but they don't believe you?

This monumental thing had happened to me, but the world didn't stop for me to catch my breath. I was still grappling with intense shame and regret, but the things I had always done still needed doing—sleeping, eating, cooking, parenting. Life goes on even when you're devastated. I got up every day and took Ryan to school. The kids and I still went on adventures, albeit without

Abigail in tow. I shopped for groceries. I cooked dinner. My outer life before and after the investigation looked the same, but inside I was so different. Before, I participated in my life with more of my whole self. After, my body participated, but my mind was elsewhere. I was in such a state of vulnerability and confusion that I had my hairdresser give me bangs.

I'd never needed people around me to feel secure. I've always been able to stand alone in a crowd of people and feel calm, but now, without Mike's physical presence, I felt unmoored. As soon as he walked in the door, I was tethered. Things that never bothered me before now made me slightly panicked and anxious. I didn't like it when people knocked on the door or when the phone rang. Even now, years later, I still don't like those things. I've had my cell phone on vibrate since January 2014, because every time I hear the generic smartphone ring, I flash back to Meredith's phone call from the emergency room. When I made a parenting mistake, I filtered them through the lens of the child welfare system to see how badly I did, and I wondered what would happen if someone heard about it and reported me. I often stopped to consider how my behavior would look to an outsider.

As days passed, I started to take small steps towards normalcy. Rather than wait for Daniel Holland to return my phone, I bought a new one so I could continue recording the lives of my children through photos and videos. That may seem trivial, but buying a new phone was a reclamation of power for me.

I reached into a deep well of resilience to guide me through those first weeks. I was wounded and recovering, but people who didn't know me couldn't have known how demoralized I was.

✍

What I didn't know then—and what would take me five more years to figure out—is that I had lived with undiagnosed PTSD since I was thirteen years old. Anybody would have a heightened stress response during a police investigation, but my reaction was greatly magnified because I was already vulnerable. I had experienced a few years of relative inner calm following my marriage to Mike in 2007, but the investigation changed that. If you have PTSD, I don't recommend being targeted by the cops.

In addition to my extensive knowledge of the inner workings of the child welfare system, I also had decades of experience dealing with people who were supposed to be nice to me but then suddenly weren't nice at all. When I came under attack, my brain and body said, "We've been here before." My well-honed fight-or-flight response kicked into high gear to keep me safe, and this can result in behavior that looks odd to outsiders.

My behavior up to this point makes more sense if you look at it through the lens of PTSD. The ability to think logically, to communicate clearly, to defend myself—all of those things were diminished when the toxic stress hit. My immediate recoil following Meredith and Holland's initial phone calls was greater than it should have been simply because my nervous system had been in hyper-overdrive for decades by that point. Floating through Walmart after the police had shown up at my house and seized my property wasn't only denial—it was the chronic dissociation that had been my constant companion throughout most of my life. And my physical health had long ago tied itself to my mental health when years of unprocessed trauma culminated in the auto-immune disease rheumatoid arthritis. There's only so much stress I can handle until my body says, "No more."

❧

After a few months, my boiling anger eventually settled instead of lying on the surface, raw and exposed. I wasn't yet at peace with the investigation, but I understood most of what had happened and that was a helpful first step. I kept walking forward until one day I could hardly walk at all. In April 2014 I was diagnosed with shingles, and my already impaired immune system responded by rendering me almost incapable of walking for four months. Stress is the main cause of shingles, and that illness set off a cascading immunological nightmare within my body.

In May my ankles started swelling the day after we attended a food truck festival in Lawrence. At first, I attributed it to uncomfortable shoes, but the swelling wouldn't go away and started to worsen. Sitting down, my ankles would stiffen, and I would have to stand for a minute or two to acclimate myself to the pain before I could begin walking again. At first, I would slowly shuffle until I could loosen up enough to walk with a somewhat normal gait. This happened every day, every time I stood up. I still went out with the kids, but I couldn't engage in the same way. Neuropathy and numbness soon set in. My right foot was simultaneously numb with nerve pain shooting up my leg like lightning. The pain was worse when I was still, so I had to wear an enormous boot to sleep.

My primary care doctor sent me to physical therapy, which didn't work. I went to my rheumatologist who told me to stop eating salt. After that lame advice, I switched rheumatologists, but appointments at the University of Kansas Medical Center weren't easy to come by, and I had to wait weeks to be seen. In the interim, I saw two different neurologists and visited chiropractors and acupuncturists to find something resembling relief. The acupuncturist gave me the most effective medical advice to improve my autoimmune condition: stop eating grains. Cutting out grains dramatically improved all my other joints but did nothing for my feet. On an extended family trip to Colorado in August 2014, I had to go to the emergency room in the middle of the night because the shooting pain had started in my left leg. Determined not to give in, the next day I plastered a big smile on my face and went sledding down an alpine slide on two hours' sleep with severe pain in my legs.

Several months later, on a beautiful Saturday in September, I attended a kayaking retreat with a friend and had a good time despite the pain. Afterwards, at home after my mother-in-law left, I felt tired and sat down on the couch. Suddenly, the room started spinning like I was on a carnival Tilt-A-Whirl. I managed to stand up and lurch towards the bathroom to throw up. The spinning was so intense that I couldn't open my eyes, and I laid down on the bathroom tile and waited for it to pass. It didn't pass. I crawled down the hallway to get my phone so I could call Mike, who was working three hours away in Wichita. He called his mom and sent a friend over. I laid on the bathroom floor for over three hours waiting for Mike to arrive back home, occasionally rising to vomit before lying back down. When Mike came home and saw me there, he said, "You have to get up."

I replied, "If I was capable of getting up, don't you think I would have done it by now?" I asked to be left there to die, but he hitched his arms under mine and dragged me down the hallway to the bed.

By the following Monday, the room wasn't spinning, but I was still a physical wreck. I didn't want to miss my long-awaited rheumatology appointment, because I was supposed to get cortisone shots in my ankles, and so Mike wheeled me from the parking lot in a wheelchair and I kept my sunglasses on in the exam room to minimize the vertigo.

On Wednesday, the carnival ride in my brain had returned, and I was back on the bathroom floor vomiting. I was so unwell that I told Mike I needed to go to the hospital. I rode with my head out the car window like a dog, got an IV bag of fluids and Valium, slept for fourteen hours, stayed in bed for two days, and started to believe that I might actually live. The time in bed gave the cortisone shots time to work and, gradually, the neuropathy, numbness, and swelling in my feet disappeared.

My body, which had kept itself together for me to make it through the active phase of the investigation, was now staggering under the weight of other people's problems and poor choices. I felt out of control. I *was* out of control. There was nothing I could do to change my circumstances because my actions didn't cause my current position. I was suffering for something somebody else did, and I had no way to rectify it. My body just kept absorbing the blows.

⁂

Later that fall, my mom called to tell me she had ovarian cancer.

By this point, I was better physically, but the ongoing low-grade stress of the case coupled with my mom's diagnosis left me with insomnia. I would wake up in the middle of the night and stare at the ceiling for hours. I engaged with the kids each day just like always, but as soon as they went to sleep, I'd disappear into episodes of *Downton Abbey* to escape.

I slowly stopped living my life, instead allowing my life to live me. Daniel Holland and Steve Holder were calling the shots. I hadn't talked to Holland in months, but I was letting him orchestrate my mind and my health like a puppeteer. I sensed the danger of becoming completely defeated and allowing Holland and Steve to turn me into somebody I didn't want to be. I didn't want to miss all the lovely things this world has to offer in favor of cynicism. I didn't want to be the person who thinks the worst about other people. I didn't even want to think the worst about Holland. I wondered about the difference between people who buckled in hardship and those who persevered. I didn't know the answer, but I knew which group I wanted to be in. Shortly after Mike and I were married, his aunt told me I was the happiest person she knew, and I wanted to find that girl and get her back.

On a whim, I signed up for online Barre3 workouts. The exercise made me physically feel better almost immediately, and I started to heal emotionally because I was taking care of my fragile body. I grew stronger, which helped my joint pain and, more importantly, the insomnia and bouts of illness stopped.

I still do Barre3 every day and eat a grain-free, mostly dairy-free, and refined sugar–free diet. This combo has worked so well for me that I was able to go off all my RA meds. Successfully managing a chronic health condition with diet and exercise is a big deal, especially when you consider that I began to feel better than I had in a decade. Before the investigation, while on medication, I sometimes couldn't lift my arms above my head or twist open a lid without assistance. Once I started barre workouts and altered my diet, I could put my kayak on top of my car. In the long run, my lifestyle changes probably saved my life, and I'm not sure I would have found my renewed health had this case not brought me so low. I have Daniel Holland and Steve Holder to thank for that. I don't believe this was their intention, but I'll take it.

⁂

As time wore on, I kept making positive choices for myself. I kayaked. I hiked. I kept sewing. I kept reading. I kept gardening. Every day I did something good to counteract the bad, but no matter how much joy I added to my days, the case was always there because I never experienced true closure. I had never been able to tell Daniel Holland and the Holders what I knew to be true. I've never cared too much what others think of me, but knowing that people still thought that I hurt a child when I didn't bothered me tremendously.

Why did I stay silent? Why didn't I say what I wanted to say to the people I wanted to say it to? Why didn't I say to Holland, "Steve broke her arm before she came over." And why didn't I say to Steve, "Tell Holland you broke her arm before she came over." I placated the system with silence and suffered for it. I didn't call attention to the wrong that had been perpetrated against me, and against Abigail. I wish I had reported Daniel Holland to internal affairs during the investigation. I wish I would have insisted that my attorneys call up the prosecuting attorney and raise hell. And most importantly, I wish I would have marched up to Steve and Meredith and said, "I know what you did. You fooled everybody else, but you didn't fool me. I figured it out."

But the system doesn't work that way. Mike would often say, "All of this is bad, but the worst thing that could happen is being charged with this crime," and so we worked to avoid that one thing. My statute of limitations wouldn't expire until December 2, 2018—five years in the future—which meant that I could be charged at any point until that date. Even though I didn't do anything wrong, accusing the investigators of incompetence when those same investigators could influence my charging decision was unwise. And I still had to see the Holders around town and say nothing. I couldn't risk making them angry and have them respond by demanding that I be charged with a crime. I had to bide my time and see what decisions strangers made about my life. This layer of helplessness was exasperating.

When I quit my job with the State, I had a vision of a certain kind of childhood I wanted to give my children. I pictured tromping through the woods, exploring trails, splashing in creeks and rain puddles, climbing trees, swimming in lakes, playing at the pool, learning to read, cheering at Ryan's games and everything else that comes with a boy's adolescence. I did not envision being investigated for felony child abuse. I decided to stay home to simplify, and then the actions of other people dumped a truckload of chaos into our lives.

I'm not sure how my response to the stress from this case impacted the people closest to me. I wonder how my kids will remember me when they think back on this time in their childhood. When I was consumed with anxiety, how did that look from their vantage point? Did I pass my frustration and anger on to them even though I tried not to? Did they think I was upset with them, when in reality I was upset with Daniel Holland and Steve? What did they think was happening when Mike and I had heated conversations about the case? What thought patterns did I incorporate into my mind and body, and in turn their childhood experiences, that I can't take back? How much of my emotional energy was taken away from my family and put towards this case? I don't know the answers to these questions. What I do know is that somebody else broke their child's arm, and my children paid the price for it.

We had other stressful life events during this time, but everything eventually resolved. This case never did. Instead of knowing when we could begin rebuilding, the case and its accompanying stress carried on and on for years. The open investigation was an unending, uncontained event that made for a shaky foundation from which to contend with everything else that happens in a family. Things weren't always at a boiling point, but I could always sense an undercurrent of stress in our lives. We would exhale during a quiet period and move towards normalcy, but then new information would crop up and we would be in turmoil again.

I couldn't direct my anger where it belonged, and since something of this magnitude has to go somewhere, I put it where anger usually ends up going: right on top of my spouse. Mike and I couldn't fight the system, so we fought each other. That's one of the worst parts about traumatic life events, isn't it? The person you need the most is the person you dump your problems onto, because you have nowhere else to put them. The pressure during this period in our lives was so profound that I sometimes didn't know if we were going to stay married. We had always looked out for each other and put the interests of the other above our own, but this case turned us into combatants. I was contending with my own frustration while in an occasional state of overwhelm, and Mike was next to me in the exact same position. Each new development in the case added another layer of frustration and resentment that we couldn't crawl out from under. We had nothing left to support the other, or build the other up. We still had good moments, but this case was a pickax chipping away at the contentment and constant respect that used to support our marriage. The actions of other people pitted us against each other in a way we never would have stooped to on our own.

⌁

When I investigated families, I often thought I understood how my actions affected them. I believed I had a grasp on how I was impacting their lives. I was wrong. My work stopped mattering to me at 5:00 p.m. because I went home to my private life. I turned work off and didn't think about it again until I needed to. The families I investigated didn't have that luxury, because their private life *was* the case. The things I did and said, the way I treated them, the decisions I made—those things impacted someone's *life*. The cases that were inconsequential to me within my bigger picture were huge to the client because the case was their bigger picture.

I was assigned at least fourteen hundred cases when I worked at DCF, and I conducted multiple interviews within each case. I interviewed so many people that I can't remember all of them. I have no idea what I said to people or how I made them feel. CPS social workers are not therapists, and we didn't have a lot of free time to spend making sure everybody felt okay. One thirty-minute conversation with a client flew out of my brain and landed with all my other nonessential memories, but that same thirty-minute conversation could have had an emotional impact on the client that lasted for years. In child welfare, it's routine to have hard and unpleasant conversations with people. The fact that tough conversations are so commonplace makes it easy for professionals to disregard how that experience might feel to the people on the receiving end.

A client I had previous history with was pregnant and due any day. Unfortunately, she was also in jail on theft charges and there was some concern that she was a sex worker. Her baby would be delivered while she was still incarcerated, but, rather than put the child in foster care, I took a leap of faith and believed her when she said her relative would be able to care for the baby while she was locked up. I made a referral to in-home therapists so they could monitor the baby's progress and keep an eye on things. I needed the mother to sign paperwork to set up services, and I arranged to meet her in the jail the day after she gave birth so that she could sign the forms. My main objective was to get the forms signed as quickly as possible and be on my way. I breezed into the jail, through the maze of corridors and locked doors, and into the area where the cells are located to wait for her in the conference room made available to us by deputies.

The mother was distraught when she came into the conference room. She had given birth the day before, and she explained that she had been transferred back to the jail, despite the fact that she wasn't scheduled to be transferred to another jail until the day following our meeting. She sobbed and kept repeating, "I could have had one more day with my baby. I could have had one more day with my baby. I could have had one more day with my baby."

I had allowed no time in my day for her feelings or any type of conversation beyond what I needed for the forms. I was in the county jail talking to a hooker, and I hadn't even taken the time to consider that she might have feelings just as valid as anyone else's. I had only allowed time for a signature. As she cried, I realized I had been in such a rush that I hadn't even bothered to sit down. I was standing over her impatiently, focusing only on myself and my plans for my day. I quietly slid down into a chair and told her it was going to be okay, an insufficient response for her situation.

When Holland was done with his interviews, he filed his reports and moved on to the next one. I wouldn't be surprised if he never thought about me again. Why would it have mattered to him? It was just another case.

Chapter 10

The Finding Letter

AFTER MY POLYGRAPH exam, I didn't hear anything about Daniel Holland until Ryan came home from school in April and said Holland had arrived at his school to speak with him.

When child abuse reports are assigned on families with school-age children, it was always our practice to speak to the kids at school without their parents being notified, because state statutes allow social workers to do so. After being assigned a report, my first order of business was almost always to drive to the school and present the school secretary with paperwork that listed the statute and the name of the child. The child was pulled out of class and brought to a private room where I interviewed them. If there were siblings, I interviewed those children too.

We did it this way because a surprise visit made the child's information more reliable. There was less chance that they would have been coached by a parent, and it was more likely that they would speak freely. It was only afterwards that I called the parent and said, "I spoke to your child at school today." Did this enrage some parents? You bet. I understood their anger, because having the State speak to your children without your knowledge can feel like a gross violation of rights. My standard explanation to parents was that some children in this world are horribly mistreated, and we never knew who those children are at the beginning of an investigation. We had to treat all families in the same way until we knew what we were dealing with.

Ryan could have been a wealth of information. He could have provided context on my mindset at that time, any comments that I had made about Abigail's injury, my temperament when I dropped him off at school. Interviewing him at school without my knowledge was a good idea on Holland's part, and I didn't object.

It just happened five months too late. Ryan's interview should have occurred in the hours or days immediately after my first interview. Ryan's information would have been more reliable had it been gathered closer to when the injury was discovered. I was suspected of injuring a young child while also being the primary caretaker of two young children of my own, and Holland needed more information about what kind of person I am. I can't think of a good reason for Holland to have waited so long to interview Ryan, who was present in school every school day from December 3, 2013, through April 2014.

April 2014 marked the first and only time that anybody working on this investigation spoke with any of my children. Nobody from the KBI or DCF ever attempted to speak to Thomas or Joseph. Not only that, but nobody even laid eyes on Thomas or Joseph. Holland speculated that I became so mad at them for running away from me that I broke Abigail's arm, but he never bothered to check on the welfare of my twins that I lived with every day. That is negligent.

~

In the summer of 2015—a year and a half since the active investigation—I received a call from a Topeka number. I sent it to voicemail, and Holland left a message saying that he had information about the case. I have no idea what I would have said to Daniel Holland had I answered the phone. Rather than call him myself, I contacted my attorney.

Holland's information was that the attorney general's office had declined to prosecute me. This was good news, but I still was frustrated, wondering if the attorney general had figured out that Abigail's injury occurred before she came over. Avoiding prosecution was good, but what I really wanted people to understand was that I didn't do anything wrong. I wanted everyone to know the truth.

The charging decision was made in June 2015, nineteen months after Abigail's injury was reported. Nineteen months after a preverbal child was determined to have a spiral fracture in her arm and immediately returned to the home of her parents. And it was eighteen months after I repeatedly told Daniel Holland and Scott Campbell that I didn't do it.

A year later, in August 2016, Mike, the twins, and I drove to Orange Beach, Alabama, while Ryan stayed home to work. We love the beach and spent the entire vacation doing whatever we wanted. On the way home, we made an impromptu stop at Fantastic Caverns in Springfield, Missouri. While waiting in line for the tram that would take us into the cave, I suddenly became agitated. I had gone from a frolicking-on-the-beach vibe to feeling like I wanted to choke somebody in a matter of seconds. *Why do I feel like this? Where did this come from?* I couldn't figure it out. Mike and I hadn't argued, the kids hadn't misbehaved, and the whole vacation had been a roaring success from start to finish.

Sensing my change in mood, Mike asked, "Are you okay?"

"No," I replied, my voice tense and strained. "I am absolutely not okay."

"Why? What happened?"

"I wish I knew." It was irrational to feel this way, but I couldn't shake it. I managed to make it through the tour without ruining everybody's time, but that black cloud stayed.

On the four-hour drive from Springfield back to Kansas, I realized that I hadn't received a finding letter from DCF, even though it had been close to three years since the case was actively investigated. Finding letters are sent to involved parties once an investigation is complete to tell the family what social services had decided. I had not been actively wondering about this and—just like my dark mood—I didn't know why it had suddenly appeared.

When we arrived home from Springfield and began unpacking our gear, I checked the mailbox which was stuffed full of back mail. My heart skipped a beat when I saw a letter from the Johnson County Kansas DCF office with the Notice of Department Findings tucked inside.

The form letter indicated that I had been substantiated for the physical abuse of Abigail Holder. An explanation of what a substantiation means was included, although I already knew. The letter read,

> If a substantiated perpetrator does not appeal or the appeal is unsuccessful, the substantiated perpetrator's name will be placed on the Kansas Child Abuse/Neglect Central Registry. Persons whose names appear on the Central Registry are prohibited by law to work, reside, or regularly volunteer in childcare homes or facilities licensed or regulated by the Kansas Department for Health and Environment.

An explanation of the definition of physical abuse was attached: "Infliction of physical harm or the causation of a child's deterioration, and may include, but shall not be limited to, maltreatment or exploiting a child to the extent the child's health is endangered."

One sentence at the bottom of the form explained DCF's

reasoning behind my substantiation: "Andrea Verbanic admitted to giving the child a 'bear hug' and hearing the child's arm 'pop.'"

I stood motionless, trying to absorb what I was reading. To begin with, I've never heard of an abusive hug. I once read a police report describing how one of my clients got rip-roaring drunk and gave "boisterous hugs" to random strangers on the street, but an abusive hug was a new one. More perplexing than that, DCF substantiated me for hugging Abigail even though hugs can't cause a spiral fracture. The finding didn't make sense. Holland's theory was never even about the hug. His entire investigation centered around the Festival of Trees. In fact, Holland and Campbell indicated that I had made up the hug, yet DCF substantiated me for hugging Abigail even though hugs can't cause spiral fractures, and I had adamantly denied that any twisting motion occurred when Abigail was in my care.

When I came to terms with the fact that I wasn't responsible for Abigail's injury, the hug and all the circumstances surrounding it faded into the background. The hug had initially loomed large in my consciousness but soon became white noise. After January 2014, I didn't think about the hug when I thought about the case, because I knew that the hug was irrelevant. My focus switched to other parts of the day that meant something, like the look on Abigail's face when Steve brought her in the door, the text message to Steve about her not eating breakfast, and her uninterest in finger painting. Those were the things that mattered because those were the things that proved her injury occurred before she arrived. I had all but forgotten about the hug, but DCF had now put it firmly front and center once again.

When I read the substantiated finding, my ability to feel any compassion for Steve hit a brick wall. Whenever I would have an angry moment over the years, Mike would explain, "Andrea, he probably doesn't know what you've been through. Daniel Holland most likely isn't keeping him updated on the progress of the case."

I agree that Steve likely never knew what my interviews were like or what Holland thought I did. However, a copy of the finding letter was distributed to Steve and Meredith, which meant that Steve knew I had been substantiated for something I didn't do. Steve may not have known it before, but he knew it now.

I often wondered how far Steve was going to let it go. What would have to happen to me for him to speak up and tell the truth? When I received my finding letter, I realized there likely wasn't a line he wouldn't cross. He never intended to save me.

I bounced around the house for a solid forty-five minutes questioning the finding, the workers, Daniel Holland, Steve Holder, and anybody else I could think of while Mike sat on the couch and listened.

If I chose to appeal the substantiation, I would be arguing with illogical people. Attempting to reason with unreasonable people who work for a government agency is often unwinnable, and I didn't know if I had the energy to go through that. Even basic communication from anybody about this case exhausted me. On the other hand, I was being blamed for something I didn't do, and this was horribly unfair. I had been placed on the Child Abuse Registry for something that had nothing to do with me.

I went back and forth between the two extremes for days. In the end, I couldn't let it go. The thought of it was overwhelming, but I decided to appeal the finding. In doing so, I knew that I would be afforded one major opportunity: The DCF case file isn't open for public consumption, but DCF would have to produce their investigative file for my review as part of the appeal process. I would finally be able to find out what Steve and Meredith said to authorities about Abigail's broken arm.

Chapter 11

The Appeal

MY FRIEND WHO worked for DCF felt so confident in my side of the story that she thought I could represent myself in the appeal. I, however, did not have that same confidence. I made a mistake by not hiring an attorney in the beginning, and I wasn't going to misjudge the situation again. Based on a recommendation from one of my criminal lawyers, I hired attorney Bailey Murphy in Topeka, Kansas, to handle my appeal.

Even though I wasn't guilty of what DCF accused me of, I know that I *appeared* guilty simply because they had substantiated me. I know that my story is unbelievable, and on the official paperwork, I look guilty. In my written case synopsis I provided to Bailey, I included my theory that Abigail's arm was injured prior to arriving at my house. I didn't have any knowledge of the investigation outside of my own interviews, but I believed the injury occurred in the morning with Steve before he dropped Abigail off.

After Bailey briefly glanced at the letter and we had time to talk about the facts of the case, she said, "In a situation like this, DCF might suggest that you participate in services like anger management. If you agree to terms like that, it might help you reach a better conclusion."

In response, all I said was, "I'm not going to agree to that because I don't need anger management. I didn't break Abigail's arm."

On August 16, 2016, Bailey formally requested an appeal hearing, and DCF was given until September 13 to produce a summary of their case. Just as I did in the immediate aftermath of the investigation, I went on with my life and waited to see what would happen next.

∽

On September 6, I accompanied my mom to an oncology appointment. Mom was lying on the exam table resting with the lights off when her doctor came in. He broke the news as gently as he could: "Mary, you are actively dying." After being told that she had two to three weeks to live, I took her home, told my dad, made phone calls to each of my family members, met with hospice to make plans for her care, and got her situated. On my drive home I had to pull over on the highway to throw up.

I'm grateful for that slow time waiting for DCF to respond. I didn't want memories of my mother's death to be intermingled with talk of Daniel Holland and child welfare services. We were fortunate enough to have six weeks left with my mom, instead of the two or three predicted. I didn't have to spend any time actively thinking about my appeal and instead focused on caring for my mom. These weeks were a sacred blessing.

Because of my mom's terminal diagnosis, DCF agreed to extend the timelines. My mom died on October 16, 2016, and was buried three days later. By Halloween, I was back in communication with Bailey about the appeal.

While I cared for my mother, Bailey had obtained the audio recordings and listened to them. She wrote that all the information gathered in the investigation supported my theory that Abigail's break could have occurred before she came over. Bailey asked me to review the recordings as well, and I was eager to do so, even through my grief.

✍

In the midst of being blamed, substantiated, defensive, and heartbroken, I still had to contend with the Holders—always the Holders. After Ryan's final high school football game on October 28, 2016 (only twelve days after my mother had died), in a large crowd of parents, friends, and football players standing at the ten-yard line, Steve sought me out. After all that had happened, the individual who had caused me immense pain and suffering was standing beside me like he didn't know I had been wrongly substantiated. Patting me on the shoulder, he said nothing of the finding letter, but instead complimented Ryan's effort throughout the season. Given the setting, I couldn't respond how I wanted to, so I simply said, "Thank you," and continued standing next to Steve as I watched my oldest child with his teammates. What else could I do?

Chapter 12

The Investigative Reports

A SOCIAL SERVICES investigation begins with the intake procedure. Child abuse reports are made online or to a hotline number, and the report is then screened in or out, depending on if it meets criteria for assignment. The purpose of the intake process is to gather preliminary information, not to make any conclusions. If the allegations in the report meet criteria to be investigated, the report is assigned to the child abuse investigation unit (where I had worked). Investigators then determine if the information in the intake is true or false.

Reading through Abigail's intake form in Bailey Murphy's office, I read that the report was made while Abigail and Meredith were still in the emergency room, but the reporter's name was blacked out (likely a medical professional at the hospital). The report contained substantive information about Abigail's state in the ER and where Abigail spent her time that day. Everything looked standard until I reached the end: *Assigned as physical abuse of Abigail by Andrea. Child sustained a spiral fracture while in the care of Andrea.*

Before Abigail left the emergency room—and before anybody else besides Meredith had been interviewed—DCF had already decided that I caused her injury.

The intake worker had more than one responsible way to handle this case: They could have listed the perpetrator as *unknown*, because Meredith's statements gave no indication of who actually caused the injury. The intake worker also could have listed all the adult caretakers—myself, Meredith, and Steve—as potential perpetrators. Either of those options would have left it up to the investigator to determine who caused the injury.

When I was employed at DCF, the investigators routinely complained about the Intake Unit. Intake consistently miswrote names and other information, and they waited hours to assign reports. I never assumed something was true just because the intake department wrote it in the report. I always figured something in the intake was probably wrong.

One day the Intake Unit was short on staff, and investigative social workers had to fill in by answering the phone. I was there for one hour, and the phone rang constantly. It was an endless loop of ringing. I didn't even have time between phone calls to make sure I had everything from my previous call typed up correctly. I did the best I could, just like the other intake workers around me. When my time was up and I was safely back within my own cube, I sent an email to everybody in my unit, plus the director of my region, explaining that I took back every bad thing I had ever said about the Intake Unit. At the end I added, "Please don't send me back there."

The Intake Unit should have done a better job assigning this case, but, to be fair, they probably didn't have the time.

◆

One of the biggest mistakes in this case—and there were several—stemmed from one line in the intake report: "Abigail will be released to her mother. Eudora Police were contacted and at the hospital while report was being made."

I understand that everybody thought I did it in the very beginning of the investigation. Even *I* thought I did it in the beginning. Circumstantially, I'm the most likely culprit. Had this been my investigation, I might have initially operated on the same working theory.

The intake form had observations about Meredith's demeanor: "Meredith seems appropriately concerned about Abigail and Meredith seems to function fine"—in other words, Meredith looks believable. Lockhart didn't speak with anybody but Meredith at the hospital, so Abigail went back to her home based only on the uncorroborated account of her mother. I cannot overstate the magnitude of this error.

In Meredith's first formal interview, she stated that she put Abigail in bed with Steve at 5:30 a.m. and made no statements about any odd behavior from Abigail. After Meredith put Abigail in bed with Steve, she left for work. Abigail was alone with Steve for two and a half hours, and Meredith acknowledged that she didn't know what happened during this time. Based only on Meredith's word—who wasn't even present with her daughter for most of the day—Lockhart decided to send a preverbal child with a spiral fracture back to her residence with no form of safety planning or intervention. Not only is this irresponsible, it can be dangerous.

Lockhart could have safely handled the situation in one of two ways on the night of December 2, 2013. The first—and best—option would have been to start interviewing relevant parties that same night, including myself and Steve. The immediacy of the interviews would have given everyone less time to get our stories straight, and investigators would have been able to ascertain Abigail's safety utilizing more complete information. If that couldn't happen because it was late at night, Meredith could have agreed to have a noninvolved party (like her mother or a friend) be with Abigail overnight until the investigation could be taken up first thing the next morning. This would ensure that Abigail wasn't being returned to someone who potentially abused her, though it would also have given all caretakers more time to plan what they were going to say.

When he responded to the Lawrence Memorial Hospital emergency room, Eudora Police Department Sergeant Victor Lockhart was the first and only investigator who made contact with Abigail on the day her injury was discovered. In Meredith's second interview, she stated, "Lockhart was unprofessional. He was already pointing fingers in the hospital. He said, 'Oh, so she got hurt at the babysitter's?' He said three or four times that nobody was worried about us."

It's one thing to make a guess based on extremely limited information. It's entirely different to tell a caregiver what your guess is before they've even left the emergency room. Right away, Lockhart told Abigail's parents they weren't going to be treated as suspects because he thought I did it. I can't imagine this didn't affect Steve and Meredith's decision-making going forward.

Eudora, Kansas, where I live and where Lockhart worked during the investigation, is a small town of about six thousand people. The small population means that the police department doesn't have specialized units like a drug unit or officers devoted only to cases involving children. In Eudora, the officer who pulls you over for speeding is the same officer who responds to the hospital when a child is injured. It's just the way it goes in small towns.

Lockhart erred when he assumed I was guilty in the ER and returned Abigail to her parents, but he was working with two significant limitations. First, Lockhart didn't specialize in child abuse cases. Second, he knew that Mike was an officer in Lawrence and that, because of the conflict of interest, the Eudora Police Department would not be able to investigate the report. He couldn't have investigated the report that night in its entirety even if he wanted to. He would have to refer the case not only to an agency outside of his own, but also outside of our entire county. He had to do something with Abigail, and it was already 9:00 p.m. Sending her home was the easiest option, especially since he had already made up his mind that I did it.

✍

Abigail went to the emergency room on December 2. Steve and Meredith weren't interviewed until December 4, the second working day after Abigail's injury was discovered. This lag allowed the Holders ample time to discuss events and get their stories straight. Meredith and Steve were both interviewed *before* my first interview.

When I was ready to dive into the investigatory materials, I arrived at my lawyer's office armed with a pen and a notepad. The secretary ushered me into an empty conference room and showed me how to access the file on the provided laptop. Settling in to listen to Steve and Meredith discuss events that had so greatly impacted my life felt borderline voyeuristic, because I doubt that they thought that what they said in private to Daniel Holland would eventually find its way to me. Listening was a weird version of time travel, because I was listening to the recordings in a time when I had already figured out what had happened, but the voices on the tape didn't know what lay ahead. I listened both as a mother whose life had been ravaged by another family, and also as a former investigator.

I plugged in my earphones, got comfortable in the chair, and pushed play on Meredith's first interview. Any fear I had was instantly allayed because right out of the gate, Meredith said, "I don't know what happened to her. I don't think Andrea did anything to her. . . . I'm confused about when or how it happened. I don't know why I didn't notice she was injured." These statements made me feel a lot better personally, but from a procedural standpoint they were also critically important. These were tone-setting statements by Meredith. The fact that the child's mother wasn't convinced I caused the injury makes it that much more disconcerting that the entire investigation proceeded with me being the only person ever considered as a suspect.

Holland asked, "Did Andrea say anything when you picked her up?"

Meredith replied, "She said she didn't eat well. She said she played with sandpaper instruments. Wouldn't that hurt her arm? But I don't know. She's so tough. She seemed a little fussy when I picked her up, but she's always fussy when you wake her up. Normally when I pick her up, she's whiny and clingy. Everything looked really normal, except looking back when Abigail plopped down and cried about her coat." Meredith felt that Abigail "seemed fine" when she left my house. Then she added, "But then again, she cried when her seat belt was put on. But sometimes she doesn't like to be buckled, so I didn't think anything of it."

Meredith continued to detail Abigail's behavior at home:

- Abigail didn't seem fussy about having her coat taken off at home.
- Abigail was fussy at home and wanted to follow Meredith around, but Meredith thought her teeth were bothering her.
- Abigail helped put laundry in the dryer.
- Abigail didn't want to be independent.
- Meredith left to take her older son to wrestling practice, which left Steve at home with Abigail.

Meredith continued with a rundown of Abigail's activities at home after Meredith returned to the house:

- Meredith didn't remember Abigail fussing over getting undressed for the bath.
- Abigail was anxious to get in the bath.
- Meredith didn't remember Abigail shrieking when Meredith took her shirt off.

- In the bathtub, it didn't look like something was wrong with Abigail's arm, but it felt different.
- Abigail only fussed when her lotion was put on after the bath, but that was not unusual.

As I listened to Meredith describe her time with Abigail, I noticed that it sounded exactly like Abigail's time with me. I felt validated because I sometimes beat myself up for not recognizing there was something wrong with her. I would think, *Why didn't you notice there was something wrong when she didn't fingerpaint? Why didn't you become more concerned when she didn't eat?* And then I would cycle into "if onlys." *If only I had noticed her favoring her arm. If only I had paid more attention.* Meredith helped me see that I hadn't missed anything at all. Abigail's behavior was so subtle that it was easy to chalk it up to teething. When a child behaves like Abigail did that day, it's perfectly normal *not* to assume it's because their arm is broken. I understood how Meredith felt. We were both working in the dark with limited information and trying to figure out what was going on. Only Steve knew the truth.

Whereas I was initially nervous to hear what Meredith would say about me and the case in general, by this time I felt encouraged about the information on the recordings. My main objective as I listened to the recordings was to gather statements about Abigail's behavior that would help prove her injury was caused before she arrived. I was pleased to be gathering information that reinforced my position and so I had relaxed considerably, both mentally and physically. And then Meredith said something that made me snap to attention.

Meredith explained that she was "overwhelmed" when the nurse at Lawrence Memorial Hospital told her that Abigail had a spiral fracture and that this is usually a result of abuse or neglect. She continued, "I wonder if it happened on Monday, or if it was something that happened before and was aggravated."

By this point I had lived for three years believing that I was the only person who had figured out that Abigail came over to my house with a broken arm. I had concluded that the only time frames that investigators or the Holders were considering were when Abigail was at my house and maybe the evening hours at the Holders'.

But now I knew this wasn't something only I had thought of. Meredith—the child's mother—spoon-fed this theory to investigators. And what did Daniel Holland and Lockhart say in response? Nothing. They asked zero follow-up questions. My focused attention moved to a unique combination of helpless frustration and incandescent rage. I now clearly understood that my life had been trashed not just by Abigail's parents but also by investigative incompetence.

I unpaused the tape and kept listening. Instead of addressing Meredith's statement directly, Holland asked, "If you were forced to say what happened, what would you say?"

Meredith replied, "I don't know. I have a hard time saying that Andrea did something, but [Abigail's] behavior was worse on Monday than on Sunday. I just think back to Abigail's behavior during the day and think something happened during the day. I wouldn't say [the injury] was neglectful or out of anger."

Holland asked, "Who do you know for sure had no part in hurting Abigail?"

This question might appear clever but is completely inadequate. Asking someone who didn't do something is much different from asking them pointedly if they did it. On face value, Holland appears to be asking Meredith if she suspects that anybody in her house caused the injury, but the question is so general that he's simply giving her an opportunity to say she had nothing to do with Abigail's injury which, of course, is exactly what she did.

"It wasn't me. She's an easy kid. Her dad for sure didn't do anything. Her brothers play with her rough . . . Jared said maybe someone was swinging her around by her arms. I asked Jared if he did that and he said no." And then, once again, completely unprompted by investigators, Meredith suggested, "I think personally that something like that could have happened in the morning before she was dropped off."

I squeezed my eyes shut, praying that Holland took the bait this time and asked her why she thought that. *Please ask her why, please ask her why, please ask her why.* In the seconds after her statement, I imagined Holland switching gears and Meredith clearly exonerating me. I waited in glorious anticipation to hear him utter the words, "Why do you think that?" but I soon came crashing back to earth. He didn't follow up. He didn't ask anything about it. The one question that would have helped me the most is the one question Holland refused to ask.

Questions Holland Could Have Asked

- What was it about the morning time that made Meredith wonder if the break could have happened then?

- If mornings are typically stressful, how does Steve respond at 5:30 a.m. when Abigail is cranky?

- What makes their mornings stressful?

- What time did the other children wake up?

- Are the older children ever responsible for Abigail's care in the mornings? What about on December 2?

- What are the temperaments of Abigail's caregivers?

- How is Abigail disciplined by other members of her family?

- What do Meredith and Steve do when they are annoyed with Abigail?
- Does anything happen in the household that concerns Meredith?

Meredith mused a little bit more about the gate incident and then said, "If she had been injured a day or two before, wouldn't we see signs? My instincts say it was at Andrea's, but I don't think it was abusive. Maybe putting her coat on and buckling her in aggravated it. A kid at my daycare broke his arm bad at the park and he didn't cry. Everybody has a different pain tolerance."

This is the third instance during Meredith's first interview where she suggests that the injury could have occurred prior to Monday. The first time she said so I was furious. The second time I was hopeful. This third time I was cautiously optimistic. Each instance ended the same way: Meredith gave Holland the answer, and Holland asked zero follow-up questions. I would walk into my first interview the day after Meredith's interview and tell Holland that Steve said Abigail had a "case of the Mondays" at 8:00 a.m. and that she didn't eat breakfast. I gave him a perfect opportunity to follow up on Meredith's idea that it could have happened prior to arriving at my house. Holland didn't mention it to me at all. In the entirety of the case, he never explored the possibility with anybody.

Holland asked if Meredith had any questions, the universal signal the interview is over. When I heard Meredith leave the interview room, I sat in stunned silence, bewildered at how close to exoneration I had been.

❦

Next up was Steve's interview. After listening to Meredith's interview, I did not expect Steve's interview to be any better. I had an uneasy feeling that it would be just as bad or worse.

Steve was interviewed immediately following Meredith. Holland started by asking, "Tell me about Abigail."

Steve gave an incredibly concise accounting of the evening that mirrored Meredith's story, and then he said, "Rewinding, I drop Abigail at Andrea's and she seems just fine. Everything in the morning seemed routine." I heard him say that and thought, *You clown!* Not only had I just listened to Steve tell a horrible lie, but I had the investigative wherewithal to understand that this lie was one of the things that helped Holland build his story that the injury happened with me.

Holland asked Steve for information about events on Sunday, and his version of events corresponded with Meredith's. The detective next asked Steve to give information about Monday morning, December 2, 2013. Steve responded, "Abigail woke up at 5:30 or 6:00. Meredith was still there and put [Abigail's] hair in a ponytail. We went downstairs for a drink and watched the news. The other kids woke up and did their routine. I got her dressed. [Meredith's son] walks and I drive the other two to school. Then I took Abigail to Andrea's. I got there between 7:55 a.m. and 8:00 a.m. I took her in and dropped her off. Monday was normal."

My co-identities as suspect and investigator crashed into each other. I heard Steve's statement about their morning routine and immediately ticked off a litany of clarifying questions that were needed. *Ask this, this, and then this. We need to know this, and also this, and then that.* Timelines are fundamental to criminal investigations. Holland allowed Steve to provide a grossly inadequate timeline. Anybody with any sort of investigative experience should recognize that.

Questions Holland Should Have Asked Steve

- What did Steve and Abigail do before the older children woke up?

- Did Abigail and Steve sit and watch the news for two and a half hours or did they do other things?

- What other things did they do?

- What time did the other children wake up?

- What is their routine that Steve referred to?

- What rooms in the house were the other children in throughout the morning?

- Who had direct contact with Abigail? When and for how long?

- Did any of the older children swing Abigail around by her arms prior to going to school?

- What kind of mood was Abigail in after Meredith left?

- Did Abigail remain cranky, or did she cheer up?

- What was Steve's temperament like in the morning?

- Is he usually on edge in the morning or is he calm?

We don't know the answers to any of those questions because Holland never asked them.

Holland followed up Steve's statement only by asking, "Did you notice any behavioral changes?" Steve said no. Holland asked if Steve had received any calls, and Steve again said no. Holland didn't know it at the time, but I would tell him the next day in my first interview that I texted Steve very early in the morning about Abigail not eating. Holland would also eventually seize my phone, and the text messages between Steve and I are listed there. He had at least two conflicting statements he could have gone back to clarify, but this was Steve's only interview.

After Steve denied the text, Holland asked, "What are your thoughts?"

"I can't pinpoint a time at our house. I don't know how it can happen. I know that grabbing can do it, but there's no bruising. She fell maybe. If there's no bruising, it has to be a fall or wrestling with a kid and nobody can identify it. If it happened with our kids, we don't let them wrestle. If it happened at Andrea's, I can't imagine it was something messed up where she was grabbed. It has to be something where she was playing with kids and got spun around. I think it was an accident."

Each parent said in separate interviews that it was possible the older children broke Abigail's arm by swinging her around, but Holland did not ask one clarifying question about it. Instead, he asked, "If it's determined that a person did it, who would not have done it?"

There's that question again, and it was no less annoying the second time around. I heard it and thought *Let me guess. He's going to say nobody in his house did it.*

"It couldn't have happened at our house. If one of the kids was playing, we would notice it. I can vouch for the people in my house. I don't like any potential accusations towards Andrea. I don't know that I've ever seen that lady angry ever." Earlier Steve had said that the break could have happened when Abigail was playing with her older siblings, but here he says that she couldn't have been injured at their house. *Which is it, Steve?*

I submitted to two interviews and a polygraph interview and exam. Steve, the other adult providing care to Abigail on the day her injury was discovered, participated in one fifty-minute interview that was chock-full of contradiction and inadequacies and ended with ten minutes of idle chatter with Holland about sports and home repair.

❧

Meredith was interviewed twice. Her second interview was on January 3, 2014, the same day Holland spoke with Mike and my friends. Meredith indicated she asked Holland for a second interview, not the other way around.

Holland opened by asking Meredith how Abigail was. Meredith replied, "I took her to the emergency room as a precaution, not because I thought something was wrong. She's not a complainer. Ryan is at our house right now. I'm bothered by not knowing what happened. A family is being scrutinized. I have pseudo guilt. We see each other everywhere. I'm wanting to know what's going on."

Holland replied with a questionable statement: "I'm trying to be objective."

Meredith replied, "There are certain things Andrea said that bother me. I'm not sure if those are real concerns or not. I feel guilty that it took so long to realize that [Abigail] was injured. Steve said, 'But she wasn't acting abnormally.' In her high chair, she just seemed like normal. Nobody in my house can come up with anything. What if it happened the day before? But it had to have happened that day."

This marks the fourth time over two interviews that Meredith questioned if Abigail's injury occurred before December 2, 2013. I started wondering if it would be worthwhile to put tally marks at the top of my notebook.

Instead of asking any follow-up questions, Holland asked Meredith to rehash the evening after she picked up Abigail from my house.

He wasn't interested in thinking about Abigail's injury

occurring in the morning, even though Meredith had now brought it up four times. Abigail's behaviors in the evening are very relevant, but not in the way that Holland thought they were. Abigail's attitudes in the evening reinforce that she behaved in the same manner throughout the entire day, and if her own parents didn't pick up on her behaviors immediately, my inability to recognize them is more understandable. Holland and I use the very same set of facts to prove two very different things.

Holland asked, "What communication have you had with Andrea since the ER?"

Meredith answered, "I feel like she's avoiding me. Does she have guilt? Does she think I threw her under the bus? Andrea seemed to love Abigail. It bothers me that she doesn't want to take a polygraph."

Holland asked, "What would you think if there was finger-pointing?" I never pointed fingers at any member of the Holder family. In fact, I did the opposite when I stood up for them. Holland was trying to bait Meredith into turning against me by lying about finger-pointing.

Meredith replied, a little defensively, "I didn't do anything wrong. It doesn't surprise me that Andrea is turning it back on us. That makes sense now why she won't look at me. I'm busy and some say too busy. It's not like I neglect my kids."

Even when Holland tried to make Meredith believe I did so, she still didn't say she thought I broke Abigail's arm. She defended herself, but she didn't implicate me.

Holland stated, "I want to close doors. Will you take a polygraph?"

Every police officer operates differently, but I'm perplexed as to why, in order to close doors, Holland focused on the polygraph exam instead of responding to the contradictions in the parents' statements. Instead of hooking the Holders up to a machine, why didn't Holland ask Meredith what made her think the injury could have happened in the morning? Why not point out Steve's inconsistencies to him and see how he responded?

Meredith agreed to take the test, but she then said, "It makes me nervous—the thought of it." She asked how it works and Holland explained it.

Meredith's next statement was unexpected, especially since it was in response to Holland asking her to take a polygraph exam:

"Lockhart is unprofessional. He was already pointing fingers in the hospital. He said, 'Oh, so she got hurt at the babysitter's?' He said three or four times that nobody was worried about us. Do you know for sure that it happened on the second? Could it have happened a day or two before? The kids helped me watch Abigail before that. Can an arm be broken if she fell while walking?"

Even after I refused a polygraph, even after Holland told Meredith the lie that I pointed fingers at her, and even after he asks her to take a polygraph, Meredith called Lockhart unprofessional for targeting me and then questions for the *fifth time* when the injury happened.

❦

I didn't listen to all of the recordings of every interview. Steve and Meredith gave more than enough information for any logical person to conclude that the investigation wasn't complete—and if it wasn't complete, then I shouldn't have been substantiated. Listening to hours of interviews where Daniel Holland asks the wrong questions (or no questions) seemed like a colossal waste of time.

Instead of listening to the entirety of my three interviews, I chose to focus on only my first interview. I was most concerned with what I said during my initial contact with investigators that reinforced my position that Abigail arrived already injured. The information I gave in my first interview about the morning at my house seemed the most pure because, at that point, I was hyper-focused on having caused the injury and had not yet realized it had occurred before she ever came over.

I pressed play with trepidation. I worried about how I would sound when I was lying. Would I sound fake? If I did sound fake, how would that make me feel about myself? Would it be hard to listen to? Surprisingly, I sounded just like myself.

After the investigation, I remembered telling Holland in my initial interview that Abigail came over with a sour look on her face and I asked what was wrong. Instead, I heard myself only tell him on the recording that Abigail looked "tired" when she came over and that Steve said she had a "case of the Mondays." I listened as I told Holland that Abigail didn't eat, that I texted Steve about it, and that she didn't finger paint. I was left wishing that I had been clearer about her behavior, or that I had provided more details. I had to keep reminding myself that, at this juncture, I simply hadn't realized that her arm was already broken when she arrived. I had done the best I could.

⁂

Recordings of Holland's interviews with Mike, Ryan, and my friends were included in the DCF file. I've never listened to them. They had no first-hand knowledge of what transpired that day, so listening to the recordings would have eaten up time I didn't want to spend in Bailey's office. More than that, I didn't want to listen to Holland talking to them. Listening to that would have made me angry—not because they might say something bad about me, but because Holland might have made them feel uncomfortable or nervous. I couldn't bear to hear it. I didn't have—and probably never will—the emotional detachment necessary to listen to that. Bailey listened to the recordings and reported that nothing in them was incriminating.

There is no record of Holland speaking with any friends of the Holder family.

Daniel Holland interviewed the older children in the Holder family at school. I've never listened to these interviews for the same reason that I didn't listen to recordings of my friends and family members. They were just kids, and none of this was their fault.

Once I saw the date of their interviews, I also assumed any information the Holder kids gave would be useless. Abigail's injury occurred on or around December 2, 2013. Despite the fact that both Meredith and Steve indicated on December 4, 2013, that Abigail could have been injured by her older siblings, none of them was interviewed until January 8, 2014.

There is absolutely no reason to wait that long to interview the siblings of an injured child. Best practice would have been to interview the Holder children at school on December 3, 2013, without alerting their parents. Interview questions focusing on their contact with Abigail the previous morning, Steve's temperament in the morning, and the morning routine would have provided a framework for the adult interviews. Children can be a wealth of information, but the longer you wait to interview them the more you risk that they will forget what they used to know. The children were not prompted to give a detailed morning timeline for December 2 in their interviews, but even if they had been, how could they be expected to remember the morning schedule thirty-seven days later, especially when those thirty-seven days included the Christmas and New Year's holidays? How could a child—or an adult, for that matter—be expected to remember subtle differences about a morning routine that occurred over a month before they were finally being asked about it? Bailey listened to the interviews and reported that one child stated, "I don't remember that day."

Even though I spent hours between my second and third

interviews going over December 2, 2013, I didn't remember something Abigail did that day until well after I spoke with my attorneys following my polygraph. Our routine when we left the house for our outing was that I walked down a couple of stairs and then called for her to come to me so I could pick her up and carry her down the stairs. Abigail always came to me whenever I asked her to, but on this day she didn't. She just stood and stared at me which was very unusual for her. I had to ask her three times to come, and when she didn't, I had to go back up the stairs to get her. She cried when I picked her up. I think by this time in the day she had figured out that it hurt when I touched her arm, and she didn't want me to pick her up because she knew it would be painful. I felt sad thinking about that.

You think you'll remember everything, but you won't. The passage of time dulls recollections and changes perspective in a critical way. Immediate interviews are so important for this very reason.

Bailey listened to the children's interviews. One child confidently stated that Abigail was hurt by someone in her family picking her up and accidentally hurting her arm. Another stated that the injury was most likely an accident and not abusive. The third child stated that he was playing with Abigail and then she was "being weird with her arm," so Meredith took her to the hospital where the spiral fracture was detected.

I don't know how these statements would have played out in Steve and Meredith's polygraphs, because January 8, 2014, the date of the children's interviews, also happened to be the day I called Holland and confessed.

❧

The DCF finding form is an internal document used by social workers to record the information gathered during the investigation and is used to make the finding determination.

DCF's log notes immediately shed light on why it took them so long to substantiate me. In Kansas at this time, DCF had thirty days to make a finding on abuse and neglect reports, but I didn't receive my finding notice until almost three years after the case had been assigned.

I knew that findings can be delayed if the social worker is waiting on information from law enforcement, such as police reports detailing statements from suspects. If DCF is not directly involved in interviews (and they weren't in my case), then social workers use law enforcement's interviews to make their finding. I had several cases where my case closure was delayed up to three years because I was waiting on law enforcement to complete their work.

DCF log notes indicated the assigned social worker repeatedly asked Daniel Holland for reports up until February 2015 so that she could use the reports to close the case. The worker logged that Holland didn't have any reports to give her. (I don't know why he said that since he had forwarded some reports to Dr. Desiree Mitchell at Children's Mercy Hospital in February 2014.) Furthermore, KBI documentation would later show that Holland's supervisor approved some reports as early as December 17, 2013. Others were approved by a supervisor in mid-January 2014. Holland had documents to share with DCF when they asked, but for whatever reason he didn't send them.

The original caseworker left the agency in February 2015, and the case was transferred to supervisor Hannah Taylor's unit that same month. The next log occurs on May 17, 2016, over a year from when the case landed in Taylor's unit. The newly assigned social worker logged that she received the event from her supervisor that day.

On May 18, the new social worker logged an email to Daniel Holland that read, "Today I was given a case to follow up on that unfortunately has sat on a shelf for over a year." I read that and thought, *Bless her heart*. Having a case file sit on a shelf unattended for over a year is cringeworthy, especially when you consider that it was sitting there, gathering dust, while Abigail resided at her home where the injury occurred. I was shocked that the social worker wrote that down until I realized that she likely did so to pass accountability from herself back to her supervisor, where it belonged. I would have done the same thing.

When the finding was finally completed, Meredith's statements were summarized in twenty-six lines of text. Steve's interview was summarized in ten lines of text. The short narratives include basic summaries of the information given by the parents. The children's statements are not included in the finding form. Neither are any statements given by Ryan, Mike, or my friends.

My interviews are summarized in sixty-three lines of text. Despite the larger space given to what I said, my statements were greatly condensed. For example, the end of my polygraph exam was outlined like this:

> Andrea was advised of the results of the examination and continued to deny any responsibility in the injury sustained by Abigail if it was not caused by either the hug or having gone through the baby gate. Andrea stated that Abigail had fallen while she was holding her hand as they walked down the street but denied such event was remarkable where such an injury could occur.

The facts are technically there, but this summary doesn't even come close to conveying how adamant I was that I didn't twist Abigail's arm, accidentally or otherwise.

The finding form quotes Dr. Mitchell, the doctor consulting on the case:

> Spiral fractures are caused by torsional forces (forces involving rotation or twisting of the bone). The force

used to cause this type of fracture is greater than what would be used in routine care of a child. This type of fracture can be caused by violent twisting or rotation of the arm. Routine hugging of a child does not cause injuries.

The last paragraph states:

Information obtained from the interviews and reports indicate that the child received a significant injury, a spiral fracture of the humerus, while in the care of Andrea Verbanic. The facts and circumstances provide clear and convincing evidence to conclude the alleged perpetrator's actions met with KSA and KAR definition of Physical Abuse.

The finding form provides no discussion of the thought process used by DCF staff that resulted in them believing I caused Abigail's injury when I hugged her, especially when they quote the doctor saying that routine hugs don't cause injuries. Just like when the DCF Intake Unit made an assumption of my guilt, the assigned social worker made a huge leap: "The child has a spiral fracture and the child was at Andrea's all day, so Andrea did it."

Early in the aftermath of the active investigation, my friend said she wished I had been honest from the beginning, as if this would have somehow changed things for me. At first I was tempted to believe that my initial withholding of the hug is what made investigators target me for Abigail's abuse, but now I know that I wasn't targeted because of that. My lie about the hug wasn't what caused investigators to determine I broke Abigail's arm. The determining factor in my guilt was that investigators decided I was guilty. When they sent Abigail home from the emergency room and reported to DCF that I caused Abigail's injury, I hadn't lied about anything because nobody had spoken to me yet. I hadn't said anything about anything to anybody but Meredith.

Had I walked into my first interview with Daniel Holland and said, "I hugged her and I think that broke her arm," the outcome of this case would have been the same. He was never going to believe my story regardless of when I said it. He demonstrated repeatedly that he wasn't willing to consider my innocence.

If Holland didn't catch on when Meredith suggested five separate times that the injury could have happened before Abigail came to my house, nothing I said was going to make a difference. I wasn't placed on the Central Registry because I lied. I was placed on the Central Registry because *Steve* lied and the investigators believed him over me.

Something this case taught me about one dangerous element of our criminal and child welfare systems is this: Once they think it's you, it's you even if it isn't you. Nothing you do or say will ever change that. It doesn't matter what you know and when you know it, or what you say and when you say it. It doesn't matter if there are conflicting statements or things aren't adding up. It doesn't even matter if there's no concrete proof that you did it. When your guilt has been decided and they're no longer entertaining any options besides you, it's over.

Chapter 13

The Reasoning

WHENEVER SOMEONE LEFT frontline social work, inevitably the workers left behind would start to view that person as being out of touch with reality. Since leaving the vanguard myself, however, I think a more plausible explanation is that the workers who left actually went *back* to reality. Child Protective Services tricks social workers into thinking that their job is reality, but it's not. The child welfare system is a parallel universe built on storm clouds of dysfunction and paranoia.

I was once assigned a report regarding a mother leaving a child in her car while it was running so that she could walk her older child into school. Even though I knew that stranger reports are rare (anybody who works in CPS can tell you that the real danger isn't strangers, it's within the child's network of family and friends), I immediately went into worst-case-scenario mode and latched on to the worst story I could think of. I wanted to document that I had made her aware of every conceivable danger to her child. I had no plans to forward the report to the police or try to have her arrested. What I was interested in was covering myself in case she left her kid in the car again.

In this instance, worse-case-scenario was Jake Robel, a child dragged to death down a highway by a carjacker when his mother left him in the car to run into a sandwich shop. I printed off a newspaper article on Jake Robel and gave it to this woman at our first interview. I didn't segue into Jake Robel during the interview. I didn't say, "I understand your decision-making process. Is there another way that we could do this that would satisfy the concerns of the school?" and then casually mention Jake Robel. I led with Jake Robel: "We received a report that you left your kid in the car. You can't ever leave your kid in the car because you could be carjacked, and he could be dragged to death like this poor child in the news." The mother looked at me like I was overreacting for comparing Jake's situation with her own.

At the time of the investigation, my interpretation of the mother's response was, "She doesn't get how serious this is, but I do because I'm a social worker and I know the way the world really works." It wasn't until I quit DCF and was separated from the chaos of the job that I realized how that conversation actually happened. I understood that my client looked at me like I was overreacting because I *was* overreacting. Who is crazier: (a) The mother who leaves her child in her vehicle in a school drop-off lane so the child isn't exposed to winter elements while she walks her older child into school, or (b) the social worker who draws a line between that action and the child in the car being dragged to death down an interstate? For current CPS workers who might be reading this, the correct answer to that question is *b*.

When you work in the system, you develop institutionalized thinking, almost as if you're thinking like the agency you work for and not like an independent person. Some social workers (and police officers and lawyers and judges) have the tendency to believe that we are all-knowing because we've seen it all. We know how a case will end because we've seen this one already. The narrative is whatever we say it is because we are The Ones Who

Know. When you are used to dropping the hammer and saying, "This is how it is because I say that's how it is," sometimes you can't recognize that your version of reality isn't how it is at all.

⁓

To any competent individual who listens to the interview recordings, one thing is obvious: nobody knows for sure what happened to cause Abigail's injury—except, of course, for the person who caused it. I know that it happened before she arrived because I lived the day, but an outsider wouldn't be able to tell when her arm was broken, who broke it, how they broke it, or whether it was abusive or an accident. Holland's investigation is incomplete. He worked one theory half to death and left all the other theories dangling in the wind.

My Steve-did-it theory is a guess, of course, just like Holland's half-baked Festival of Trees scenario. But my theory is at least backed up by actual statements given by the child's caregivers and not the result of my imagination working overtime. Even though the interviews were mishandled, Holland still had more than enough information available to narrow down the timeframe for Abigail's broken arm:

- Both parents agree that Abigail didn't exhibit concerning behavior on December 1, 2013, even in hindsight.
- Meredith stated that she put Abigail in bed with Steve at 5:30 a.m. on December 2 and that she "didn't know what happened after that." Meredith made no statements about any odd behavior that Abigail exhibited at 5:30 a.m., even in hindsight, so we can guess that she was not injured at 5:30 a.m.
- By 8:00 a.m. on December 2, Abigail was noticeably upset when she entered my house.

- If she showed no signs of injury at 5:30 a.m. but was cranky at 8:00 a.m., we can conclude that her injury could have occurred somewhere between those times.

Now that we have the time*frame*, the time*line* of events between 5:30 a.m. and 8:00 a.m. becomes critical. If Holland had ascertained who had contact with Abigail, when, for how long, and what they did together, that would help us narrow down the perpetrator. Holland's ineptitude lost us that information forever.

At a minimum, after all the initial interviews were complete, Steve should have been treated as a potential suspect. If nobody ever bothered to ask Steve if he caused Abigail's injury, how do we know what his answer would have been?

≈

Neither Meredith nor Steve ever expressed any anger towards me. Even when they made suggestions that I caused the injury, they expressed no hostility. On the contrary, they talked about what a nice person I am.

Abigail's parents should have been at least mildly upset if they believed the babysitter broke their baby's arm. The fact that they weren't should have piqued Holland's interest. My speculation regarding their lack of anger? Steve knew I didn't do it because he knew he did, while Meredith was hesitant to believe that I caused the injury because of activity in her own home.

Meredith even went so far as to send the email to Holland asking why I was being targeted:

> I just don't understand why it is seemingly being assumed that Andrea harmed her. . ... If she did something wrong then yes, I would be glad that the KBI would've prevented any conflict of interest issue, but at this point I don't see what evidence anyone has that would cause Andrea to be

the prime suspect in causing Abigail's injury. Andrea is a caring and stellar individual.

Abigail's own mother could see a lack of evidence connecting me to the crime.

❦

Any investigation is chock-full of lies, minimization, scandal, and fragmented clues. Investigations are hard, but they become much harder when you decide what happened at the beginning of the case and ignore everything that doesn't support your theory.

You might be surprised to learn that what happened during the active phase of this investigation isn't the thing that concerns me the most. The interviews were horrendous, of course, but I'm more than willing to concede that mistakes happen. What really scares me is everything that came after.

PART TWO

CHAPTER 69

Chapter 14

The Letter

I WAS SUMMONED to the office of the regional director one day towards the end of my career. My instinct was to believe that I was in trouble, but someone else was in trouble and I was going to be the one to clean it up. Another social worker was going through a challenging time and had stopped making timely contact with her clients, something that is a really big deal within child welfare. I was given a stack of her files and instructed to follow up on all of them to verify what had been done (or not been done) and then complete the work. I wasn't told to limit the damage or lie, cheat, and steal to get our agency out of trouble. I was only told to fix what went wrong.

On almost every case, the clients verified that the social worker had not interviewed them. One mother I spoke with confirmed that the worker had spoken with her and instructed her to keep her child away from his father until the social worker investigated and determined it was safe for the child to return to his father. Unfortunately for the family, the social worker didn't do any more work on the case—and the instructions were issued three weeks prior.

When I found out that a father hadn't seen his child in three weeks because of the actions of one my co-workers, I was appalled. I wasn't upset at the social worker, necessarily, but at how the agency I worked for had upset the dynamics of a family in a way we shouldn't have.

I hung up with the mom, placed my telephone headset back in the cradle, swiveled in my chair to grab my purse, walked at a brisk pace out the door, and pulled out of the parking lot almost on two wheels to get to the child's school so I could ask him about his dad. The boy gave no reason for the father to be kept away from his child, and I called both parents and explained that. I was as nice about it as I could possibly be. I told them it was wrong for it to have taken this long. Afterwards, I emailed the regional director and said, "I fell all over myself apologizing to the family. I think I smoothed it over." She didn't ask me if there was going to be fallout. She didn't ask if we were going to get sued. She said something along the lines of, "Good," and that was that.

When you find yourself in this kind of mess in child welfare—and if you stick around long enough, you will—this is just how you're supposed to do it. There's nothing special about how we handled this because when you are the cause of a problem, it's basic manners to fix the problem.

✦

Bailey suggested writing a letter to DCF detailing my position in the hopes that they would reverse the finding decision without having a hearing. I was grateful for a concrete task to direct my energy and attention. The investigation was so bad that DCF had to understand what happened when I told them.

I didn't know exactly how DCF decided to substantiate me, but I felt confident that no one listened to the recordings. I don't remember ever listening to a police officer's recorded interviews when I was employed at DCF because police interviews are often long, and I was always short on time. When I made a finding based on information gathered by law enforcement, I reviewed only the police reports that summarized the recordings, assuming that all relevant information had been included by the officer. If I needed clarifying information, I called the officer and had that person answer my question in their own words rather than listen to the recordings.

∽

After emailing back and forth, Bailey sent me a draft of her letter to DCF for my approval. In her draft, Bailey only offered as an alternate hypothesis the fact that Abigail could have been injured by her siblings during rough play and said nothing of the possibility that Steve could have done it. I pushed back and insisted that she include the possibility of Steve's involvement.

At first Bailey wasn't sure if including my theory was a good idea:

> Sure I can add the alternate theory. I hadn't gone down that path originally because there wasn't any testimony or other evidence that suggested it. I didn't want it to detract focus from the other supported theory. We can put the alternative theory out there as secondary to the first theory and make the argument that we'll never know because of the shoddy investigation. Of course, the slight risk in this case is that DCF staff go back and reinterview Steve to cure the alleged defects.

I didn't want to leave Steve out of it simply because Holland didn't collect enough evidence. If anything, I felt the lack of information was one compelling reason why the State shouldn't have substantiated me. The investigation was woefully incomplete.

The threat of Steve being re-interviewed didn't scare me, but

I was concerned about *how* they would re-interview him. I worried that a re-interview might be a staff member calling Steve and asking, "Andrea says you broke her arm before you dropped Abigail off. Did you?" Then when Steve said no, they would check the box indicating that he was asked the question and move on.

∽

Bailey and I came at the case file from different angles. I listened for statements that bolstered my belief that Abigail arrived already injured, and Bailey concentrated on someone who I had almost completely ignored but who was actually critical: Dr. Desiree Mitchell, a physician at the Children's Mercy Hospital SCAN team, a group that focuses exclusively on child abuse cases. DCF used Dr. Mitchell's medical opinion in their finding, and Bailey recognized much earlier than I did the impact that the physician had on my case.

Bailey grouped her letter into different areas of concern, each under a different bolded, underlined heading. She hit all the high notes, including Abigail's behavior throughout the day and at night, the sibling theory, the Steve theory, Meredith's email to Holland, and Holland's procedural mistakes (including questions he should have asked but didn't). Bailey included time stamps whenever she referenced a comment from one of the interviews so that DCF could hear the statements for themselves. In the end, she brought all of it together to explain that Dr. Mitchell was given incomplete information that impacted her medical opinion, in turn impacting my finding. The letter ended with a request to dismiss the finding against me and enter a finding of an *Unknown Perpetrator*, meaning that the injury was likely the result of abuse, but nobody knew who caused it. This was my idea. I thought it gave DCF an opportunity to dismiss the finding against me while also not having to go back and reinvestigate something that happened three years earlier.

I loved Bailey's letter at the time. The recordings backed up my position so completely that only a fool would be unable to see the error in DCF's case. When I read the letter now, after I know DCF's response to it, I wonder why I ever thought it was going to work. Bailey used facts and rational arguments to fight against an agency that didn't appear to value either. I was wholly unprepared for how DCF responded to Bailey's letter; although, with the way this case had gone since the beginning, I should have seen it coming.

✍

The first meaningful communication from DCF came on January 17, 2017, when DCF attorney Kelly Anderson emailed Bailey to ask for a continuation. DCF wanted to communicate with Dr. Mitchell about Bailey's letter and review the evidence. Bailey told me that she thought this was a good sign and an indication that we had opened up a different perspective on the case. I was slightly less positive given my recent experience with DCF, but we agreed to the continuation.

Communication about this case was hard to handle because I never knew when it was coming or how bad it was going to be. I would be involved in the ordinary events of my life when *bam!* an email would land in my inbox. It might be minor information that I could easily cope with, or it might be so stressful that it completely derailed me for hours, or even days. I never knew which one it would be. On February 13, 2017—nearly a month after they had asked for a continuance—I was in the middle of preparing a snack for my kids when my phone alerted me to a new email from Bailey.

She first explained that Dr. Mitchell rejected the plausibility that an older sibling swinging Abigail would have caused the injury. That news wasn't so bad because I had also rejected the sibling theory. Then Bailey wrote that Dr. Mitchell remained steadfast that the injury occurred when I hugged Abigail and heard her arm pop. A wave of anxiety coursed through me: butterflies in my gut, coolness throughout my body, a rapid heart rate. I briefly thought, *How is this possibly happening?*, but my confusion and frustration were quickly replaced by blind fury when I started reading what was attached to Bailey's email: DCF's log notes.

The first set of log notes were written by DCF supervisor Hannah Taylor, who was tasked with contacting Dr. Mitchell about the new information in Bailey's letter. I recognized Hannah's name from when I worked at the agency but didn't know her personally, and this was the first I was aware that she was involved in my case. She logged that she read page seven of Bailey's letter to Dr. Mitchell, and the remainder of the log listed Dr. Mitchell's response in a bullet-point format. Every line evoked a visceral response from me.

- "Andrea admits she was frustrated and took Abigail and gave her a bear hug and heard a pop. Doctor states the child's arm broke at this moment." *I wasn't frustrated when I hugged her! I didn't say that! I didn't break her arm when I hugged her!*

- "Doctor said a hug or bear hug of normal force would not cause her arm to break, even if it was somehow behind her back." *Then why are you saying that I broke her arm when I hugged her?!*

- "Andrea also stated she feels terrible she broke her arm." *But I only said that in the beginning! I only said it one time! Then I told Holland over and over that I didn't break her arm!*

- "Doctor notes the mother said the child's arm was bothersome to the child when mother arrived to pick her up from Andrea's in attempting to put her coat on." *No, she didn't! Meredith didn't say that!*

- "Doctor said by Andrea's own statements she fed Abigail breakfast, had yoga time, and music time without the child remaining fussy." *What?! I said she* didn't *eat breakfast!*
- "Doctor stated she reviewed a video KBI showed her in which Abigail was playing the bongo drums during music time with both arms and there was no sign of injury. Doctor said with the injury/broken arm the child would not have been able to use that arm as depicted in the video." *But she* did *play the bongo drums with a broken arm! She was upset before that even happened!*

Every bullet point was like a punch in the gut. Just like DCF's initial finding notice, I had a hard time figuring out what was going on. I read Hannah's log notes and thought, *What are these people talking about? None of this makes sense.* One of Dr. Mitchell's statements confirmed what I believed to be true about the older children not being responsible for the break, but the rest of her interview ignored almost all relevant facts of the case. It was like she was inventing her own reality, but the most frustrating part was that Hannah didn't correct her flawed assumptions. For every point Dr. Mitchell made, Bailey provided a counterargument, and many of them came with a time stamp so they could verify the information in the recording. Per her own log notes, Hannah Taylor didn't push back against Dr. Mitchell with any of the facts laid out by Bailey. Dr. Mitchell made statement after statement that the recordings refuted. She was basing her medical opinion on misinformation and flawed assumptions, and Hannah Taylor let her do it.

I was still standing frozen in the exact same spot in my kitchen when I flipped the page from Hannah's logs to Teresa Walker's, an employee from a different DCF region who was assigned to review the file with a supposedly objective eye. My internal dialogue while reading Hannah's notes centered around rebutting Dr. Mitchell's flawed statements. My inner discourse while reading Teresa's notes more closely resembled what you would hear in an old-school girl fight at a high school football game.

- "In review of the evidence, the child was healthy and appeared to be in no pain when she was dropped off at the babysitter's home." *Whoa, Teresa. Slow down. What evidence are you talking about? Refer to the text message I sent to Steve, Teresa!*

- "During her polygraph, deception was noted, Andrea stated she broke the child's arm, Andrea stated she gave the child a 'bear hug' and heard a pop, she feels that is when the child's arm broke." *This was true one time, Teresa. One time! You know what else is true, Teresa? That I repeatedly denied breaking her arm after Holland said hugs don't cause spiral fractures.*

- "DCF obtained all the information from KBI to include audio recordings of interviews and phone calls." *Wow, Teresa. Just wow. Obtaining recordings is a solid first step but do you know what the real objective is, Teresa? Listening to them. It doesn't matter if you collect audio recordings if you never listen to them.*

- "No reports or allegations the injury occurred at the mother and father's home." *Teresa, you are blowing my mind. Did you miss the part in Bailey's letter where* her parents *said the injury could have happened at their house?! That didn't jump out at you?*

- "DCF and KBI were thorough in interviews." *OMG Teresa, what are you talking about? Do you even know what you're talking about?*

- "I did not see any interviews or information which were missing." *For starters, how about a timeline of morning activities at the Holder residence on December 2? That was conspicuously absent. How about that, Teresa?*

Later I'd wonder if anybody even gave Teresa a copy of Bailey's letter. Maybe Teresa Walker wasn't ignoring facts. Maybe Teresa was simply unaware of the facts, which would put her in the same group as almost every other person involved in this investigation—with the exception of Daniel Holland. Maybe she was just trying to work a puzzle with half the pieces.

To this day, I've never been able to understand why DCF sent us Hannah and Teresa's log notes. They detailed work product so poorly executed that when I read them, I felt like I was in possession of something I shouldn't have—like a damaging internal memo that was stolen by a rogue employee and handed off to a reporter in a parking garage at midnight. I'm not sure if everybody working at DCF was unaware that what they did demonstrated a complete lack of critical thinking skills or if they just didn't care.

❧

I remember everything about recording the bongo drums video on December 2, 2013. The drums were sitting on my lap because I played them first. Abigail tottered up to where I was sitting on the couch and hit the drums several times with both hands. I thought, *She is so precious!*, and I figured it would be a perfect video to send Meredith to show her what Abigail was up to. I grabbed my phone and instructed Abigail to play the drums again. I leaned back against the couch and filmed while she hit the drums with both hands. She looked content and very pleased with herself, and I thought that would be a very good thing for a working mom to see. It was a sweet little moment. I didn't know at the time I hit "send" that it would eventually become a large part of my undoing.

Teresa, Dr. Mitchell via Hannah, and even Lockhart way back in the emergency room each said something along the lines of, "I observed the video of Abigail playing the bongo drums in the morning with no apparent injury to either of her arms." Following this logic, if her arm didn't look broken when she played the bongo drums in the morning and then she cried uncharacteristically when Meredith put her coat on, I had to have broken her arm sometime between the bongo drums video and 4:45 p.m.

I don't blame anybody for looking at the video and thinking Abigail's arm wasn't broken. Even I had a hard time with it between my second and third interviews because she looks so obviously unharmed. However, when you look at the video in the context of all the other statements about Abigail's behavior during the day by both her parents and myself, it becomes easier to see how she would have played them with a broken arm. But for the video to be looked at in context, Dr. Mitchell and Teresa would have had to have all the information.

Hopeless frustration started to set in again. Convincing anyone that Abigail's arm was already broken in that video would be difficult.

❧

Bailey gave me two choices in how to proceed: I could drop the appeal and allow my name to be placed on the Child Abuse Registry. My other choice was to go forward with a hearing. Bailey laid out an estimate of costs associated with a hearing, which included paying $300–$500 an hour for an expert witness to contradict Dr. Mitchell's medical opinion. Bailey felt that Dr. Mitchell could be attacked by her misunderstanding of certain facts, namely her belief that Abigail was asymptomatic when she arrived and that Meredith noticed her injury immediately upon picking her up.

The amount of money I had paid out to Bailey Murphy up to this point was $7,000. This was in addition to the $1,750 I paid my criminal attorneys and the $600 I paid for a new phone. I was growing increasingly bitter about the amount of money we were shelling out to defend myself against something I didn't do. Every check I wrote made me angry because it was money I was spending on someone else's family. And even if you're lucky enough to win an appeal, the State doesn't refund your money. It's not like returning faulty merchandise at Walmart and producing your receipt at the customer service desk to have the money credited back to you.

One could argue that the hearing officer on DCF appeals is supposed to be objective and impartial. And who else is supposed to be objective and impartial? Law enforcement and DCF staff. Nobody working on my case up until this point had given me any reason to believe that I was going to get a fair shake in a hearing. I wrote to Bailey, "The hearing officer is supposed to be impartial, but I have been assigned the world's biggest idiots at every phase of this case and I don't have high hopes that he's any smarter than they are."

I could have chosen to spend thousands of dollars on an expert witness to contradict Dr. Mitchell. I could have paid Bailey Murphy hundreds of dollars an hour to cross-examine every assumption that Dr. Mitchell and DCF staff made. I could have chosen to do all of that, and I still could have lost.

I was in an unwinnable situation. Unless someone were to admit their role, no one could say with any certainty who caused Abigail's injury. If I couldn't prove who did it, I wouldn't be able to prove I didn't.

Nobody was going to believe that Abigail came over already injured unless Steve said she did. I didn't think Dr. Mitchell was going to change her mind without Steve being honest, and I didn't think Steve was ever going to be honest. I could attempt to refute Dr. Mitchell's opinion with another expert's opinion, but her opinion was still going to be the one used by DCF in their defense of the finding. If DCF had Dr. Mitchell, they were going to win the appeal. I wouldn't be able to win without Steve, and I was never going to have Steve.

I knew I was right. I knew I didn't break Abigail's arm. I knew it happened at her residence prior to her arriving at my house, and I knew the investigation conducted by the KBI was frighteningly inadequate. I also knew that none of that seemed to matter to DCF based on their correspondence with Bailey. Refuting Dr. Mitchell's mistaken assumptions about Abigail's behavior throughout the day was easy because it simply involved pointing out statements from Abigail's own parents. Convincing people to believe me was the hard part.

Bailey told child welfare officials there was a wealth of information on recordings they had in their possession indicating Abigail was abused in her own residence and their response was, "We are simply unable to alter the finding based on the additional evidence." That is arrogance. They knew they could do whatever they wanted because they made the rules. Who was going to stop them?

Aside from the money and my belief that the appeal was likely unwinnable, I had to consider my health. I am very susceptible to stress-induced RA symptoms because of PTSD, and DCF's response to Bailey's letter sent me over the edge. I was sitting on the love seat in my room one evening when I suddenly experienced the all-too-familiar rheumatoid arthritis stiffness radiating through my body. It crashed into me and sent me into a flare-up that lasted for days. I was on my way to being back on my bathroom floor.

I didn't rush into my decision, but I felt intuitively that dropping the appeal made the most sense for me. I wanted the truth, and continuing to fight DCF wouldn't give me that. I wanted to know what happened to Abigail, who did it, and who let everybody think it was me when it wasn't. Holland kept badgering me to be 100 percent honest, and the irony is that nobody wanted the truth more than I did. Dropping the appeal was my white flag. My beloved mother—who I had spoken to every day for decades—had died, my health was failing yet again, and I was exhausted. I didn't want to fight anymore.

On February 28, 2017, I emailed Bailey and told her I wanted to drop the appeal.

Chapter 15

The Aftermath, Part I

BEING ON THE Child Abuse Registry doesn't affect your livelihood if you're a mortgage lender, because the activities the Registry prevents you from doing aren't things you would do anyway. But I am a social worker, and being on the Registry was going to matter to me in a monumental way. Securing a job in the social work field is almost impossible if you're on the Registry because it shows up on background checks. It's hard to get a job in *any* helping profession if you're on the Registry, and helping professions are where my talents and interests are. I wanted to go back to school to get my master's degree in social work, but practicum sites do Registry checks and so I had to forego that.

When I dropped the kids off at school in August 2017, I suddenly had hours of free time and no way to fill them. I didn't volunteer in their classrooms because I wouldn't be able to pass a background check if the school requested one. This would have been humiliating for me and would have placed a label on my children, so I stuck to sending napkins to holiday parties. I wanted to find a part-time job, but trying to come up with ideas for employment left me completely frozen, mainly because I couldn't find anything that I had experience in or desire to apply for.

Mike suggested I become a bank teller, but I cried panicked tears when the teller in the informational video started counting the money. I can barely add, and the thought of being responsible for someone else's money was too much to bear. I thought I could deliver Amazon packages. I would be great at that, but no one responded to my application. I tried to stock shelves at Walmart—because I truly love Walmart—but they didn't call me back either.

My unemployment was a stressor in my life over the next couple of years. It wasn't about the money, necessarily—although a second income would have been nice—but more about the fact that I wasn't in control of my own life. I didn't get fired from one job—I was fired from an entire field, the only field I had any desire to work in. Not only was I paying a price for something I didn't do, I now didn't even get to make decisions about how I used my strengths and talents. I couldn't make my own plan for which direction to go, and that frustration and resentment sometimes affected how I showed up for my family.

There will always be a huge question mark surrounding Abigail's injury and, in turn, my involvement in it. I will likely never be completely absolved of responsibility because of the nagging doubt in people's minds that I did it. At the time I made the decision to drop the appeal it came down to this: I didn't value DCF's opinion of me more than I valued my health and my sanity. I set a boundary on how far I was willing to go and how much I was willing to give of myself, and I've never regretted it. My body is a faithful barometer by which I can monitor how well I'm living my life and, going forward, I never had another PTSD or RA flare about this case.

❧

Two months after I dropped my appeal, on April 17, 2017, Mike walked in the door from work and said, "I saw Kelly Anderson today." I was confused, because Kelly, the DCF lawyer handling the appeal, was a direct player in my life but not necessarily in Mike's. "She showed up at work with her husband to witness the promotion of another detective."

Mike explained that Kelly's husband was introduced at the ceremony as working for the Kansas Bureau of Investigation after previous employment as an officer in Leavenworth, Kansas. Mike remembered Daniel Holland telling him during his interview that he also worked as an officer in Leavenworth prior to working for the KBI.

A quick Facebook search revealed that Kelly Anderson and Daniel Holland were friends. I don't know how close they were or the nature of their relationship, but the fact that Kelly's husband worked for the same agency as Holland did not bring me comfort. Bailey's letter that detailed various procedural flaws with the investigation and discussed Holland's tunnel vision was received at DCF by Holland's friend, a DCF staff attorney married to a KBI agent. Kelly Anderson was also involved in the initial staffing that led to my substantiation.

Small world, isn't it?

A couple of my friends were fired up over the news. A third friend had no adverse reaction because she admitted to not being surprised by anything at this point, and I felt the same. This case was a morass of foolishness and silliness from the moment it began, and so, by this time, it would have been more of a shock to me if the lead investigator and the DCF attorney *weren't* friends.

When you work with people, you will likely be friendly with them. I have lasting friendships from my time at DCF, and I developed friendships with people who worked in other community organizations. Sometimes people took it a step further and married people from other agencies. Mike and I were two of those people. We met at work and eventually married, so I recognize the interconnectedness of life in the system. This doesn't have to mean that your work product will suffer.

I don't generally have a problem with people within the system being friends with each other so long as everybody acts right. The problem I have with Holland and Kelly's friendship is that I don't think anybody ever acted right on this case. Just because you are friends doesn't mean you're out to bamboozle people, but when the investigation involves some questionable business, the ability of individuals to manage their opinions and friendships becomes a concern. We tend to believe our friends more than we believe strangers. If DCF would have done a more thorough review of Daniel Holland's case (including comparing his written reports with the recordings) I might believe Kelly and Holland's friendship was irrelevant. But DCF didn't do that, so I can't help but see their relationship as suspicious and shady.

When writing reports, social workers get to portray people and families in whatever way they see fit, and others will believe them because they're social workers. You have the client's version of reality and the social worker's—and those two things aren't necessarily always going to be the same thing. It's not that the client's opinion about their behavior doesn't matter; rather, the social worker's opinion can matter more. The same is true with cops. Who are most people going to believe: the police officer or the criminal?

I felt a deep sense of peace about dropping the appeal, but I was still bothered that I never got to tell my side of the story. Up to this point, everybody else—from the Holder family and the Eudora Police Department to the KBI, DCF, and Dr. Mitchell—had written my story for me, and they had made me out to be someone I wasn't. Bailey's letter was my legal defense, but it wasn't my story. Bailey understood what had happened, but my story deserved my own words.

I didn't know how to remedy this situation, so I did what I always do when I need to figure stuff out: I spent hours sitting quietly on the love seat in my room talking silently to myself— *How do I fix this? What do I do? What next steps do I take?*—and waiting until I could feel the answer. I knew that defending myself in an appeal hearing was not the right choice for me, but letting the State think all those wrong things about me didn't feel right either. After weeks of rumination, I finally landed on a decision: I would write my own letter directly to the State defending myself in my own words. I wasn't trying to win anything or change anybody's mind. I simply wanted my own voice included in my file so there would be a record of it when I applied to have my finding expunged from the Child Abuse Registry in three years. I planned to expand on Bailey's letter, send it to DCF, and then move on.

~§~

In my letter to DCF I intended to include a clear statement that I did not twist and/or break Abigail's arm; why I initially thought I did and why I chose to lie about it; why I dropped my appeal; Dr. Mitchell's flawed decision making; the fact that children are capable of performing activities with broken arms; the lack of exploration into morning activities at the Holder residence; and the absence of a morning timeline. I wanted my letter to be as factual as possible, so I drove to Topeka a couple of times to check what I was typing against the recordings to make sure I had things right.

Throughout my conversations with Bailey Murphy in late 2016 and early 2017, I asked her several times where Holland's police report was in the file so I could read it. She and her assistant responded that there was no police report included in the file. This was very odd because case files always included a police report, and I didn't know how Holland would have avoided writing one. Without a police report, I didn't understand how DCF obtained their information to substantiate me. During a trip to Topeka on March 29, 2017, to do research for my letter, I happened to open a file on the computer that I had missed by initially focusing almost exclusively on the recordings. It contained Holland's police reports, but they were labeled "Written Summaries."

The appeal hearing officer had issued an order that I wasn't allowed to take any of the documents from Bailey's computer to my own residence or email them to myself. I didn't have time to read the police reports in Bailey's office because I needed to get back to pick up the kids from preschool. In the interest of time, I took pictures of each page on the computer with my cell phone before I left to drive back home.

I had a few spare minutes waiting in the hallway for the preschool door to open, so I started thumbing through my pictures of Bailey's computer screen. Surrounded by other mothers chatting idly about their kids, I propped myself up against a wall in the corner and began to read. I randomly started with the written summary of my second interview with Daniel Holland. The details were sparse considering how long the interview was, but one thing stood out to me. Daniel Holland wrote (italics are mine), "Verbanic said she does not know why she thinks she thought it was important to let people know that *she was angry that day*, she said it was frustrating trying to get through the gate but it was not enraging, she was not furious and they got through the gate and it was fine."

What I actually said on the recording was (italics are mine), "I don't know why I'm so focused on people knowing *I wasn't angry that day*. I think it was kind of frustrating going through the gate but it wasn't enraging. I wasn't furious. We got through the gate and it was fine."

The low murmur of happy conversation in the preschool

hallway was in direct contrast to the darkness of what I was reading. Holland wrote in the police report of our conversation that I said I *was* angry when I had said that I *was not* angry. The wrongness of what he had written hit me hard, but it also provided clarity to something I couldn't figure out during the appeal: the State and Dr. Mitchell kept referencing me being angry.

The State social worker wrote that I was angry going through the gate in the initial finding form. Dr. Mitchell told Hannah during the appeal that I was frustrated when I hugged Abigail and that she believed this is when her arm popped. In Teresa Walker's review, she wrote twice that I said I was angry that day.

Each time I read this during the appeal I told Mike that I didn't understand why they kept saying it. I knew I wouldn't have told anybody I was mad because I wasn't mad that day. Back in the preschool hallway, I kept staring at the words "was angry" on my phone thinking, *Is this real? Am I imagining this?* I thought perhaps I was not reading it correctly because what Holland had written was not accurate, and surely there wouldn't be such an obvious inaccuracy in a police report. To check myself, I texted a screenshot to my friends and asked, "Does that actually say *was* there?"

I believe in giving people the benefit of the doubt. Maybe Holland made a typo. Maybe he really did misunderstand me, but when it came to Daniel Holland and everything that had led me to this point, I had a hard time believing anything but the worst-case scenario.

In the initial meeting with my criminal attorneys in 2014, they explained that Daniel Holland was likely going to make me look as bad as he possibly could in his reports. I understood that, but I thought he would stick to a modicum of human decency and at least report the truth. As the door to the preschool room opened and the children rushed out holding their artwork from the day, I looked at that one word in Holland's report and thought, *What an asshole.*

Chapter 16

The Analysis

ONCE I HAD the kids situated at home after school, I shut myself in the bedroom and did a cursory read-through of the rest of Holland's police reports before I had to put dinner on. Even the quick scan was enough for me to develop a clear understanding of how DCF arrived at their finding that had previously eluded me. Turns out I wasn't the only one who withheld information.

For someone hell-bent on proving my guilt—as Holland appeared to be—the cornucopia of statements on the recordings pointing to my innocence would be a problem. Holland had a solution for all those pesky exculpatory statements: He omitted them. I'm not talking about one small misrepresentation here and another one over there. Holland left out every statement that gives even a small indication that I might be innocent, and then he gave those reports to DCF and Dr. Mitchell, who, in turn, used them to blame me for something I didn't do. The interplay between Holland's police reports and Dr. Mitchell's medical opinion is complex and overwhelming.

This newfound information was a game changer for me. It was bad enough that he massacred the investigation, but writing misleading police reports took it next level. After dropping my appeal, I had made up my mind that I was going to say my piece to DCF simply to have my story included in my file for my expungement request. After reading Holland's written summaries, I was no longer content with that. I was still within the statute of limitations, but what Holland did was so egregious that it compelled me to advocate for myself. He was so bad it made me bold. I determined to compare every one of Holland's written summaries with what was actually said on the recordings, which I would then put up against Dr. Mitchell's medical opinion, other medical reports, and the DCF file. And when I was finished, I was going to bypass Hannah Taylor and Kelly Anderson and go directly to the DCF secretary to request that my finding be overturned.

I had next to nothing. I had no power—Holland and DCF had all of that. I had no integrity because I lied once to protect myself, and now everybody thought I was a liar even though I was the only one being honest. What I did have was the truth, a seven-year-old iMac with some busted off keys, and a big mouth. I intended to use all of that to the best of my ability.

My new plan meant more trips to Topeka to comb through the file. Bailey's office in Topeka was thirty to forty minutes from my house depending on traffic. I'd drop the twins off at preschool at 1:00 p.m. and drive to Topeka while Mike took off work at 3:30 p.m. to pick them up. I would get as much done as I could from 1:45 to 5:00 p.m., and then make arrangements to go back again on a different day.

During the appeal when I was listening to the recordings for the first time, I drove back from Topeka each day in a rage. When I say rage, I mean talking-to-myself *rage*. Driving back to Eudora on I-70, I would say something out loud about the recordings, imagine what Holland or DCF staff would say in response, and then respond to their comment I had just made up. I was having imaginary conversations with people while driving my

2006 Dodge minivan 75 mph on the interstate. I felt unhinged. But now that I had found Holland's reports, traveling to Topeka was a different experience. Focus replaced fury. Instead of having rage-fueled imaginary conversations with Daniel Holland and DCF that played into my despair and frustration, I turned on Britney's "Work Bitch" and, with righteous indignation, nodded my head along to the beat.

Way back on February 14, 2014, Dr. Mitchell wrote a four-and-a-half-page medical opinion—excerpts of which I had previously read in the DCF finding—that I located at the same time I found Holland's written reports. At the beginning of her report, she lists the records she received and reviewed, and she relies heavily on these documents to write her own report. My polygraph interview and exam were not among them. She discusses the injury and paraphrases Holland's police reports before stating that she believed I was the one who broke Abigail's arm. Dr. Mitchell gave a very clear outline of how she approached this case when she wrote, "With the information that is available to me at this time, the history is most consistent with the arm fracture having occurred while in Ms. Verbanic's care as Abigail was asymptomatic prior to arrival and had new/acute symptoms noticed by mother at the time of pick-up from daycare." As someone with knowledge of what was actually said during the interviews, I found many discrepancies with what Dr. Mitchell believed to be true.

I have some street cred when it comes to cops and social workers. Since I'm going to discuss Dr. Michell's medical opinion in detail, I want to be completely clear about my skills and knowledge as it pertains to the medical field: I have none. When I accompanied my mom to doctor's appointments, the oncologist regularly referenced body parts I didn't even know I had. I used to ask Mike about once a year if I have a prostate because I always get it confused with the pancreas. If you're having a medical emergency and I'm the only one in the room with you, you're probably not going to make it. While I lack medical prowess, I do have common sense and critical thinking skills, and even a medical degree can't compensate for the lack of either one of those.

Behavior In the Morning with Me

When trying to determine when a preverbal child is injured, you have only their behavior to reference. When was she cranky, and when was she not cranky? When did she favor her arm and when did she not favor it? When did her behavior change, and what activity was she engaged in right before the behavior change?

How did Dr. Mitchell arrive at the conclusion that Abigail wasn't injured when she arrived? She read it in Holland's reports.

What Dr. Mitchell wrote:	What Holland wrote:	What Holland omitted:
"Parents report that Abigail had been in her normal state of health when she was dropped off at her daycare provider's home. Daycare provider confirmed that Abigail was doing well when she arrived at her home on 12/2/13."	"According to Verbanic, on 12/2/13 at approximately 8:00 a.m., Steve Holder dropped off Abigail at her house."	I said: "I could tell she was a little tired. Steve said she had a 'case of the Mondays.'" I said that Abigail cried when Steve left, which she had not been in the habit of doing.

What Dr. Mitchell wrote:	What Holland wrote:	What Holland omitted:
"Ms. Verbanic reports in her initial interview with KBI Special Agent Daniel Holland that Abigail arrived to her home at 8:00 a.m. She gave her breakfast and changed her diaper."	"Verbanic fed Abigail applesauce and toast for breakfast."	I said Abigail didn't eat breakfast and instead "just sat there."

Holland omitted details about Abigail's countenance and suggested that she ate breakfast, leading to Dr. Mitchell's narrative that Abigail wasn't injured when she arrived. Unfortunately, I didn't say that. Dr. Mitchell should have considered other references listed in the reports about Abigail's behavior during meals throughout the day:

What Lockhart wrote:	What Holland wrote that Meredith said:	Text conversation between Steve and me at 8:30 a.m.:
"Meredith told me that about 4:30 p.m., she arrived to pick up Abigail and that Andrea reported general fussiness and a lack of appetite. Meredith stated that she attributed this to teething."	"Verbanic told Meredith that Abigail did not eat well that day, and Abigail is normally a very good eater."	Me: *Did Abigail eat breakfast already or is she just on a hunger strike?* Steve: *She hadn't eaten yet this morning.* Me: *I did get her to eat some applesauce but the toast was rejected.*

To be fair to Holland, it is not his fault that Dr. Mitchell chose to focus on one line in his report of my first conversation with him and disregard the rest. To be fair to Dr. Mitchell, sifting through all the information in various reports and comparing them is challenging. Sorting through all these documents was difficult for me to do, and I have investigative experience. She read a statement attributed to me in which I said that Abigail ate breakfast. If it was written that I said that, why would Dr. Mitchell think it didn't happen?

Because no one provided Dr. Mitchell the polygraph report, she couldn't have read what Scott Campbell had to say: "Verbanic stated that she was unsure as to whether Abigail had been fed so had given her some toast of which she did not eat. Verbanic stated that she sent a text message to Steve Holder inquiring if Abigail was on a hunger strike as she was typically a good eater."

Dr. Mitchell also considered Abigail's participation in our morning activities as evidence that she was asymptomatic prior to arrival.

What Dr. Mitchell wrote:	What Holland wrote:	What I said that Holland omitted:
"The children then participated in activities such as yoga, finger painting, and music time."	"After the diaper change, the kids did some yoga, then finger painting."	I had to position Abigail in downward-facing dog because she couldn't do it herself. Abigail didn't finger paint.

Just like with breakfast, the way that Holland worded his report makes it sound like she fingerpainted and was behaving normally, but that's not what I said.

The Bongo Drums

Dr. Mitchell referenced the bongo drums video several times in her written report and in her interview with Hannah. Specifically, she used the bongo drums as proof that Abigail's arm wasn't broken in the morning.

What Dr. Mitchell wrote:	What Dr. Mitchell told Hannah:
"At 10:32 a.m., Ms. Verbanic sent a video to Abigail's mother of Abigail playing the bongos using both arms per her report she had no sign of pain or discomfort at this time." "Daycare provider . . . even took a video of Abigail playing bongo drums using both arms with no sign of pain or distress at approximately 10:30 a.m. that morning."	"Dr. stated she reviewed a video KBI showed her in which Abigail was playing the bongos during music time with both arms and there was no signs of injury. Dr. said with the injury/broken arm the child would not have been able to use that arm as depicted in the video."

Dr. Mitchell was wrong (as doctors sometimes are). A child with a broken arm actually can play the bongo drums without showing signs of an injury. This is true because Abigail came to my house with a broken arm and then played the bongo drums, and neither I nor anybody else who watched the video noticed anything wrong.

Three points of interest from the interviews could have affected Dr. Mitchell's opinion had Holland had included them:

- Meredith stated Abigail's arm didn't *look* different during her bath (which occurred around 7:30 p.m.) because her arms were chubby. Meredith stated that it only *felt* different, which caused her to initially believe it was a spider bite.

- Meredith stated five times across two interviews that the injury could have occurred before Abigail arrived at my house.
- Statements by myself and Meredith indicating that Abigail was a tough little kid.

Even with the limited information she had to work with, I've often wondered how Dr. Mitchell felt comfortable stating so unequivocally that Abigail's arm wasn't broken when she played the bongo drums. In her interview with Hannah Taylor, Dr. Mitchell didn't leave much room for doubt. I would have had a hard time countering Mitchell's medical opinion on the bongo drums, except that my son Thomas once had an incident that proves what kids can do with broken bones.

About two years after Abigail's broken arm, Mike built a treehouse in our backyard complete with a trapdoor, porch, climbing wall, rope ladder, and zip line that sent the kids from the tree house porch across the yard to another tree. It was just as fun as it sounds. On May 5, 2017, while I was working on my letter for DCF, Thomas, not content to use the zip line as it was intended, decided to go at it backwards. After a running start on the ground, he planned to swing on the zip line, bounce off the handle of the shovel he had staked in the ground at the midway point, and catapult himself onto the treehouse porch. It was a bold and imaginative strategy. He never made it past the shovel.

I was running an errand, but Mike was in the backyard laying sod when Thomas fell off the zip line from a height of four or five feet and landed on his right side. I returned in time to see Thomas sitting under a tree holding his arm and crying that it was broken. His arm didn't seem to be injured—it wasn't swollen and he had full range of motion—so I told him that was enough crying, and we carried on with our evening.

For close to two weeks, Thomas would occasionally say that his arm hurt, but we dismissed it because he fully engaged in all his regular activities with no problems. His arm also looked completely normal with no bruising or swelling. Thomas played in a soccer game the day after he fell. He played in three T-ball games over the next two weeks—one of which was five days after he fell—and in two of those games he played pitcher, repeatedly fielding the ball and throwing it to first base with his right arm. He also batted using both arms in all three games. Almost every morning for those two weeks, Thomas and Joseph would dribble basketballs or pass the ball back and forth to each other in the driveway.

Thomas climbed up the rock formations at an arboretum using both hands to balance his weight. Mike has a video of Thomas swinging across the monkey bars using both arms. He used his right hand to practice writing every morning during the week without complaint. Ryan pulled each of the twins up in the air by their hands while playing with them and Thomas laughed and did not complain. As has been their habit since birth, Thomas hit Joseph with his right hand on a regular basis with no complaint. He climbed trees nearly every day.

Thomas went to preschool five times within those two weeks, and his teachers noted nothing concerning except that he once whined after falling off a beanbag. His teacher mentioned that it was odd that he said anything about it because he normally didn't complain about falling. Right after I picked him up that day, he took off his ice pack and climbed a tree outside the school.

Thomas ran wild at Ryan's high school graduation party on May 13, including going down the zip line with his cousins. Around forty people attended and nobody noted anything wrong with him.

On May 15—ten days after the failed catapulting attempt—Thomas fell down in his room and then ran crying into the kitchen. He said, "My arm is broken! Take me to the doctor so she can fix it!"

I asked, "When did your arm start hurting?"

"When I fell off the zip line the first day Daddy was laying sod." Soon thereafter, I observed him using his left hand to eat his lunch when he didn't know I was watching.

Starting to be concerned, I texted Mike, *I think there might actually be something wrong with Thomas's arm. He just fell and now he's eating with his left hand. Do you think it could actually be broken?*

Mike said, *How could it possibly be broken? He's been walking around like that for two weeks.*

Could it just be bruised? I wasn't worried before but now I am a little.

Make an appointment with the doctor. I'm sure he's fine, but an appointment will make you feel better.

I called our family doctor right away and explained the fall off the zipline to the nurse. I said, "Thomas insists that it's broken but I don't see how that could possibly be true considering how he's been using it normally for this long.

She replied, "Sometimes it happens that kids break a bone and we don't realize it for a few days." She suggested I bring him in for a check-up, and I scheduled for later that afternoon. About two hours before the appointment, I shot a video of Thomas dribbling a basketball with his right hand.

Thomas exhibited full range of motion during the doctor's exam. He had no reaction when she touched his arm except to acknowledge that it was painful when she touched the sore spot. The doctor said she thought it was likely just bruised but, to be sure, she sent him down the hall for x-rays. To my great surprise, the initial x-ray showed a fracture. Initially, it looked like a small break on the edge of his radius, so I thought perhaps it wasn't a very significant break. While I waited for follow up instructions to see an orthopedic doctor, Thomas and Joseph took turns throwing themselves against the wall in the hallway for fun.

On May 19 Thomas had another x-ray at an orthopedic office that showed he had broken his radius straight through. It wasn't a small little crack on the edge of the bone like I initially thought. This was a complete break. By this time, it had been broken for so long they didn't even bother putting a cast on it.

Thomas was five when he broke his arm and was able to clearly tell everybody how it happened. If Thomas had been non-verbal and couldn't tell you when he broke his arm, you would never, ever, ever look at the videos of his behavior for the two weeks after his fall and think that his arm was broken. In fact, you would look at them and think it couldn't have been broken.

In her report, Dr. Mitchell wrote that Meredith and Steve noticed pain and swelling at home and then continued, "These symptoms are consistent with the type of fracture that Abigail had as movement of her arm would have caused her pain." Abigail's fracture was likely painful to her since she whined or cried throughout the day at my house when I touched her arm. While a broken arm is certainly painful, it's the *reaction* to the pain that matters. Anybody who watched Kerri Strug race down the runway, fly off the vault, and land on her broken foot in the 1996 Olympics knows that to be true. Don't we all know adults who handle pain well and others who can't handle any type of pain? I know adults who have gone about their regular business for days with an undiagnosed fracture, and I also know adults who are incapacitated by a minor head cold. Kids aren't any different. When I shared Thomas's experience with other parents, I'd hear variants of a similar story. Kids don't always respond the way we think they should. Abigail didn't.

Dr. Mitchell formed her opinion on what Abigail could and couldn't do with a broken arm based on the information she received from Holland. But if Steve had admitted breaking Abigail's arm in the morning, would Dr. Mitchell have consented that Abigail could have played the bongo drums with a broken arm? She would have had to, then, right?

This case hinges on the medical opinion of a doctor. Unfortunately for both Abigail and me, Dr. Mitchell's opinion was wrong.

Pick-up with Meredith

Dr. Mitchell was under the mistaken assumption that Abigail behaved abnormally immediately upon pick-up from my house, which we know isn't true. I have added italics throughout this section for emphasis.

What Holland wrote about pick-up from Meredith's first interview:	What Holland wrote about pick-up from Meredith's second interview:	What Lawrence Memorial Hospital Physician Assistant Maya Nelson wrote about pick-up:
"Meredith stated that when they were getting ready to leave Verbanic's home, she went to put on Abigail's coat. Abigail *whined a bit* and did not want to put her coat on."	"Meredith said that when she was putting Abigail's coat on and tried to put Abigail's right arm in the coat, *Abigail sat down and cried.*"	"Mother picked up daughter from babysitter tonight around 4:30 p.m. Mother reports patient *cried and sat on floor* when putting on jacket, but mother thought patient was just fussy due to teething/cold symptoms."

Meredith's description across three interviews as written by Holland and Maya Nelson are the same: Abigail whined or cried and sat on the floor when her coat was put on. Dr. Mitchell's report, however, describes the scene quite differently.

What Dr. Mitchell wrote:	What Lockhart wrote:
"Initial signs of pain occurred at daycare provider's home when mother tried to put Abigail's coat on. When mother went to put Abigail's arm in her coat when they were getting ready to leave, Abigail *screamed in pain* and sat on the floor."	"Meredith stated that when Abigail turned her arm to put it into the coat, she *screamed in pain* and sat on the floor. Meredith said that this confused her, but she got the coat on and went home."

Why did Dr. Mitchell write that Abigail "screamed in pain" if the three reports used distinctly different language?

If Lockhart recorded his interview with Meredith in the emergency room, I did not observe it in the file. I don't know exactly what Meredith said to him. Four different versions exist of Meredith's statement about putting on Abigail's coat, and Lockhart's is the only one that says Abigail "screamed in pain." Maybe Meredith said that to Lockhart and to no one else. Maybe Lockhart wrote what he thought he heard, and what he heard wasn't actually what Meredith said.

Meredith made two notable statements during her interviews that would have provided valuable context for Dr. Mitchell had they been included in Holland's reports.

What Holland omitted from Meredith's first interview:	What Holland omitted from Meredith's second interview:
"Now I can say it probably hurt, but at the time I just thought she was fussy. It's not like she shrieked."	"I don't remember her being in pain. In hindsight, I remember that it was strange that she fussed [about her coat] but sometimes she does."

Dr. Mitchell did not have access to the recordings, so I can't fault her for not knowing the full extent of what Meredith said about picking Abigail up at my house. However, Lockhart's report is the only one that says that Abigail "screamed in pain," and this is the report that Dr. Mitchell chose to cite in her letter.

At Home in the Evening

The evening pick-up wasn't the only time Dr. Mitchell chose to focus on the worst description available to her. She did the same thing regarding Abigail's behavior in the evening.

What Holland wrote about Meredith's first interview:	What Holland wrote about Meredith's second interview:
"Meredith said that things were normal with Abigail at home other than she was fussy, but Meredith thought it was because Abigail was teething."	"According to Meredith, when they got home, Abigail continued to be fussy and Meredith gave her some Tylenol because she thought it was because Abigail was teething. . . . Meredith stated she noticed something was wrong with Abigail's arm when she was giving Abigail a bath around 7:30 p.m."

Holland didn't include Meredith's statements that Abigail wasn't fussy about having her coat taken off, or that her whining occurred during activities that she had whined about previously, or all the times that she didn't cry when different people touched her arm, or that she didn't cry when she was undressed for bath time. At the same time, he did accurately summarize that things at home were relatively normal and that Abigail's injury wasn't detected until her bath. On this subject, his reports could have been more detailed, but they weren't awful.

Additional information from the emergency department supports what Holland wrote, but Dr. Mitchell follows Lockhart:

What Maya Nelson wrote:	What Dr. Mitchell wrote:	What Sgt. Lockhart wrote:
"Mother reports when giving child bath around 8/8:30 p.m. tonight, noticed swelling around elbow/distal upper arm area on right. Mother reports child might have been bitten by an insect or spider. Mother reports became concerned when patient had 'painful cry' when attempting to put arm into pajama sleeve. Mother reports, 'Looking back, I did notice that she wasn't using her right arm to play and pick up drinks but didn't think much of it until I noticed swelling during her bath.'"	"When they arrived home, Abigail was not her normal self. She was not happy and playing with toys. Mother also recalls, looking back, that Abigail was asking to be lifted into things that she is normally about to climb into."	"Meredith said that when she got home, she noticed that Abigail was not as active or as happy as usual and that she fussed around not playing with toys. When Meredith left to take another child to wrestling practice, Abigail was asking to be lifted into a high chair. Looking back, this was strange because Abigail is able to climb into the seat by herself."

Despite the consistency of Meredith's statements to Holland and Maya Nelson, Dr. Mitchell again went a different way. Why does Dr. Mitchell's version differ from Holland's and Maya Nelson's? Once again, it's the report from Lockhart.

Lockhart's version implies that Meredith became immediately suspect of Abigail's behaviors once they arrived home, but this is not accurate. Across her formal interviews, Meredith repeatedly stated that she was able to put the pieces together later, but she didn't see them as they were happening. Lockhart's report is again the outlier, but Dr. Mitchell chose to solely focus on it and cite it in her own report.

The ER

The portion of Dr. Mitchell's report that focuses on Abigail's behavior in the emergency department is strictly medical. She pulls from the Lawrence Memorial Hospital reports, which means that Holland and Lockhart aren't involved in any of this. Dr. Mitchell is on her own.

Dr. Mitchell wrote:	What LMH PA Maya Nelson wrote:	From the DCF Intake Report in the "child functioning" portion:
"In the Lawrence Memorial emergency room the provider notes that Abigail's arm is swollen, tender to palpitation, and has limited range of motion."	"The degree of pain is minimal."	"Abigail cried while being x-rayed at Lawrence Memorial, but otherwise is quiet and seems to function normally."

How are Abigail's behaviors at the hospital any less relevant than the fact that she played the bongo drum ten or eleven hours earlier? Abigail had a full day of activities at my house. I made no special allowances for her arm because I never knew anything might be wrong with it. I picked her up, I took her shirt off, I put her in and out of her car seat, I carried her up the stairs with my arm wrapped around her body, and I hugged her.

Abigail was seen at the ER around 9:00 p.m. If Abigail's pain was described as "minimal" and she was "functioning normally" that late in the day, she could have played the bongo drums at 10:30 that morning with no apparent difficulty.

The Hug

In Dr. Mitchell's letter, she writes, "The force used to cause this type of fracture is greater than what would be used in routine care of a child. Routine hugging does not cause injuries. Andrea's use of the term 'bear hug' indicates that more than a routine hug occurred."

What Holland wrote that I said:	What I said and Holland omitted (italics are mine):
"After they got through the gate Verbanic put the bags down and Abigail was still crying so Verbanic took Abigail to the spare bedroom and gave Abigail a big 'bear hug.'"	"I put the stuff down, and she's still mad. I take her back to the spare bedroom because she was crying and I'm going to talk to her and whatever. *I have done what I'm about to tell you a million times to my own kids and to her.* I gave her a bear hug."

Daniel Holland wrote almost all of what I said but omitted the sentence, "I have done what I'm about to tell you a million times to my own kids and to her." This omission took away the context of the hug and allowed Dr. Mitchell to instead focus on mechanics.

I used the term "bear hug," to describe *how* I hugged her, not *how hard* I hugged her. In her report, Dr. Mitchell quoted the dictionary definition of *bear hug*, a "strong and rough hug." Dr. Mitchell should have paid more attention, however, to the way I described the hug than she did to the dictionary. She didn't know how I described the hug, though, because Holland didn't tell anybody that part.

What I said about the hug that Holland omitted from his report:	What Dr. Mitchell wrote about the hug:	What Dr. Mitchell wrote about the injury:
"My initial thing was that couldn't possibly have done anything. I didn't squeeze her until she couldn't breathe. I didn't squeeze her any harder than I've squeezed my own kids a million times."	"Ms. Verbanic's history of causing the fracture by giving her a 'bear hug' with her arm behind her back is highly concerning for use of excessive force."	"Spiral fractures are caused by torsional forces (forces involving twisting of the bone)."

Dr. Mitchell felt that more than a routine hug occurred, but the two omitted statements indicate that my hug was just that: routine.

If Abigail had a compression fracture, Dr. Mitchell should have been concerned that excessive force was used when I hugged her. But Abigail didn't have a compression fracture. Abigail had a spiral fracture. Per Dr. Mitchell's own statement, torsion is needed to cause a spiral fracture and there is no torsion in a hug.

Everything that Holland omitted is important, but the most influential bits—the ones that were the most damaging—surround my confession.

What Holland wrote that I said:	What Dr. Mitchell wrote:
"Verbanic does not think what she did was abusive; she was not angry at Abigail, she was not punishing Abigail, she was not disciplining Abigail; it was nothing like that. Verbanic stated, 'But at the same time, I broke her arm.'"	"Andrea says that she feels terrible that she broke Abigail's arm."
"Verbanic feels absolutely terrible that she broke Abigail's arm; and she said nothing about it for five weeks. Verbanic said that when she was making decisions about what she was going to say, her main concern was her family. Verbanic stated that she consciously made a choice not to say anything."	

Not one of my denials made it into Holland's reports. He didn't write about my confusion surrounding the popping sound, that I denied ever twisting her arm, or that I started to believe that I didn't break her arm after being told that hugs don't cause spiral fractures. He only wrote that I said I did it. If the police officer in charge of the investigation only quoted me as saying I caused the injury, why would anybody reading those reports ever consider the possibility that I didn't break Abigail's arm?

According to Daniel Holland, I said I was guilty and never denied it.

Scott Campbell's report of my polygraph exam concludes after he wrote that I asked to speak with Daniel Holland. There is one line at the very end of Scott Campbell's report that says, "Verbanic asked to speak with Special Agent Holland at approximately 12:50 p.m. The interview concluded at approximately 1:30 p.m."

I did not locate a report of what transpired when I spoke with Daniel Holland at the end of the polygraph. Those two little sentences written by Scott Campbell are all there is. If Daniel Holland wasn't inclined to write down anything I said about denying responsibility for Abigail's injury, there would have been nothing for him to write about regarding the conversation we had at the end of the polygraph. All I did during that time was tell Daniel Holland that I didn't twist her arm and I didn't know how her injury occurred.

Making Stuff Up About the Hug

Dr. Mitchell wrote something in her report that was so confusing I had to reread it multiple times over several days and break it down line-by-line to figure out what was sitting wrong with me about it.

"Spiral fractures are caused by torsional forces." *Twisting causes spiral fractures. I get it.*

"The force used to cause this type of fracture is greater than what would be used in routine care of a child." *I agree with this. It seems like you would have to twist pretty hard to break a bone.*

"This type of fracture can be caused by violent twisting or rotation of the arm." *I agree with this one too.*

"A bear hug is defined as a 'strong and rough hug.'" *That's not how I hugged her, but okay.*

"If history is true as reported, a moment of torsion occurred." *She just lost me. What is she talking about? Why did she just say that?*

"Another possible mechanism of injury could be violently pulling and twisting an arm behind a child's back." *Dr. Mitchell, what exactly do you think you're doing?*

Part of Dr. Mitchell's job is to describe how confessions jive with injuries. Everybody agrees a bear hug doesn't involve twisting and therefore can't cause a spiral fracture and so, to make my actions medically consistent with Abigail's injury, Dr. Mitchell needed a scenario that involved me twisting Abigail's arm. She didn't have one, so she made one up. Investigators only said I admitted to hugging her, and *Dr. Mitchell* then suggested I violently pulled her arm behind her back. Cherry-picking facts out of police reports is one thing. Fabricating scenarios is quite another.

I couldn't determine if Dr. Mitchell was implying that I violently pulled and twisted Abigail's arm while I was hugging her, or if she was suggesting that I twisted her arm behind her back separate from the hug. How do you simultaneously violently pull and twist a child's arm and hug them? I'm not sure it's possible to violently pull and twist an arm while you've got both of your arms wrapped around both of the child's arms and the child is lying on a bed.

Dr. Mitchell should have given an opinion based on the information I gave and left it at that. What Dr. Mitchell should have written is, "Torsion is needed to cause a spiral fracture. There is no torsion in a hug. Therefore, the hug did not cause Abigail's broken arm." That would have put Holland in a position where he would have to go back and do more work to figure out what happened. Instead, she allowed Holland to continue to blame me for it.

In addition to omitting the five times Meredith speculated that the injury occurred prior to Abigail being dropped off at my house, Holland omitted every reference Meredith and Steve made to their children possibly having caused Abigail's injury. Instead, Holland only wrote that Meredith and Steve indicated they didn't know how Abigail sustained the injury.

Holland did not include any statements from the Holder children indicating they believed Abigail's injury could have been the result of one of her older siblings playing with her. His interviews of the children only include statements indicating that they didn't know how the injury was caused.

Holland quoted me as saying I broke Abigail's arm, didn't include any of my statements where I said I didn't break her arm, and then omitted every other alternate hypothesis given by Abigail's family.

In their reports, Daniel Holland and Scott Campbell did not include statements I made to them about having rheumatoid arthritis. If Dr. Mitchell had known I have a chronic pain condition that made it hard for me to pick Abigail up with my hands, would she have doubted my ability to twist a child's arm hard enough to break it?

Daniel Holland omitted every statement Steve and Meredith made suggesting they didn't think I caused the injury. Dr. Mitchell did not indicate that she received a copy of Meredith's email to Holland, so she probably had no way of knowing that there was a point in time where Meredith advocated for me by suggesting she didn't believe I broke Abigail's arm.

&

I once worked a case with Detective Len Bennett from the Lawrence Police Department that involved an allegation of a young girl being molested by her stepfather. I interviewed the girl, and she denied any abuse had occurred, even though every single thing about her demeanor indicated her stepdad had molested her. We were incredibly frustrated because her stepdad was a member of a notorious family of child molesters who were very good at eluding conviction. We could never quite get enough information for charges.

Len interviewed the stepdad, and at some point in their conversation, Len told him that his stepdaughter gave information about sexual contact that she hadn't actually said. When Len took a break in the interview and came into the audio room where I was watching, I told him that the girl hadn't given that specific information.

Len replied, "Yes she did. She said that."

"No, she didn't."

"Yes, she did."

"No, she didn't."

"Yes, she did."

I shrugged, "She didn't, but okay."

Later in the day when I was back in my cubical, my phone rang and Len was on the other end. He said, "I went back and watched the tape and she didn't say that. I'm on my way to apologize to the stepdad at the gas station where he works."

Cops are allowed to lie to suspects in interviews, and so technically Len was in the clear. Plus, even though the girl hadn't disclosed sexual abuse, the man was a morally deficient human being and Len didn't owe the guy anything. I don't know what kind of mental gymnastics you go through to psych yourself up to apologize to a child molester in a gas station, but I do know that Len values his integrity enough that he chose to correct his mistake when he realized he got it wrong.

When your case is assigned to a police officer, you might get someone like Len Bennett. Then again, you might not.

Chapter 17

The Report

I WAS INVOLVED in a custody case where children were caught between a mom with a meth problem and a dad who had the temperament and emotional maturity of a three-year-old. The situation was so bad that the mom's boyfriend was the most logical and level-headed of the bunch, and he was a felon several times over. I was subpoenaed to court to testify about the family in their private custody hearing. I had a no-holds-barred approach to testifying, especially in divorce-custody hearings. My objective on the stand was to get as much of my information as I could on the record until somebody told me to shut up.

On this case, I laid out both the positives and the negatives each parent brought to the table. I didn't side with one parent or the other, but instead presented the facts and explained how each parent contributed to the issues surrounding the children. I discussed what each parent was good at, and also what each parent was not very good at. When court was over and the judge returned to chambers, the mother and her boyfriend approached me and thanked me for being fair. They had just sat through a court hearing during which I had clearly stated their failings as caretakers, but they were able to recognize my fairness. People appreciate being given a fair shake, even if what is being said about them isn't all that easy to listen to. In my time at DCF, I learned that you can say just about anything to just about anybody as long as you say it in the right way. People will often know your intentions.

What Daniel Holland did in his police reports was unfair. He used his reports to shape the narrative of the case by including the statements that made me look guilty and omitting all the statements that indicated my innocence. Put together, Holland's reports show this story: Abigail was uninjured when she arrived at my house, proven by the fact that she ate breakfast, did yoga, finger painted, and played the bongo drums. I got angry going through a baby gate and responded by hugging her and breaking her arm. Abigail's injury was noticed by her parents at home in the evening. I admitted breaking her arm, and no other possibilities for her injury were offered.

I think Holland saw it like this: I abused a child, lied about it, came up with a lame story about how her arm was broken as a cover up, and refused to take responsibility for my actions. Nobody likes the kind of person Holland thought I was. His idea of justice was to omit all statements from his reports that proved my innocence and then give those reports to people who were making decisions about my life. In this way, Daniel Holland starts looking less like a gallant knight on a white horse and more like a man who has a fundamental misunderstanding of his job description.

When compared with the recordings, Holland's version of events is nowhere near the truth. He was incredibly intentional in the things he chose to leave out, going so far as to write statements almost verbatim but leaving out one sentence that cast doubt on my guilt. I've wondered what Holland's reasoning was for writing his reports in this way, but I can't come up with a scenario in which what Holland did is the right thing to do. Although police reports aren't a literal transcript of the interviews, they should still be an accurate summary of all information provided. A police officer gets to write whatever he or she wants in the reports, but I can't figure out how anybody benefits when the reports are misleading and the wrong person gets blamed for the crime. Why bother writing reports if they aren't going to represent events accurately?

Recordings and police reports aren't public record. You can't walk into the library to check them out on loan. While I think this is good protocol, this confidentiality also means that when the police act in an unsavory way, the public are unlikely to find out about it. My case was mishandled, and the only reason I know is because DCF staff substantiated me for something I didn't do, which, in turn, gave me access to Holland's reports and recordings when I appealed. Without the substantiation, I wouldn't have known how badly Holland misrepresented information in his reports. I wouldn't have known there was something in them that I needed to see.

We find out about some bungled cases when they go to court and defense attorneys tell us about it. But how many cases are like this one—mismanaged but then shelved after no charges are filed? What would we find if we always compared written reports with audio recordings? Would the written reports always be an accurate representation of what was said by those who were interviewed? More alarmingly, what about interviews and contacts that aren't recorded? If an officer writes it, people believe it—even if that officer didn't get it right.

Holland's reports are filed in whatever database the KBI uses to keep track of them. The DCF finding that lists me as a substantiated perpetrator is filed electronically in a state-wide system, which allows any employee to look it up. Years from now, anybody reading Holland's reports or the DCF finding will conclude that I broke Abigail's arm. Considering the information included in those documents, why would they think anything else?

Holland's hypocrisy was not lost on me. He repeatedly accused me of not being 100 percent honest and then turned around and wrote reports that were only about 50 percent accurate. He didn't lie, exactly, but he didn't tell the whole truth either. At what point do lying and not telling the whole truth become the same thing?

My initial lie about the hug was a big deal for the professionals on this case. My omission was mentioned as evidence of my guilt because guilty people lie. If that's being held against me, then what about Holland and what about Hannah Taylor, the DCF supervisor? I withheld information about the hug to obtain the outcome I wanted. Holland and Hannah withheld information from Dr. Mitchell to obtain the outcome they wanted. We all provided economic versions of the truth to achieve our objectives. Holland and Hannah aren't different from me. Holland and Hannah are the *same* as me, so how is it that my omission is used as evidence of my guilt, while theirs is viewed as part of their job?

We say that we value honesty, but do we really? Holland and Hannah never rectified their half-truths. Holland never wrote a report that told the whole truth, and Hannah never gave all the case information to Dr. Mitchell. Neither of them divulged what they were hiding. I did, and then I found myself on the Child Abuse Registry. The only one who told the whole truth is the only one who experienced consequences, while the ones who continued to withhold continued to get paid. Everybody who worked on this case—from Victor Lockhart to Daniel Holland to Hannah Taylor and on around to Dr. Desiree Mitchell—posed a higher threat to Abigail's safety than I ever did. Their actions and decisions resulted in a preverbal child being left at her residence, where the injury occurred, for years with no intervention. I hugged her, but I'm the one deemed to be unsafe around children.

A notorious client in our town was reported to have burned her child with an iron. The DCF office agreed that the assigned social worker did a terrible investigation and let the woman get away with intentionally burning her child. Shortly thereafter, I was assigned a case where an elementary school girl had a burn mark on her forearm alleged to have come from her sister's curling iron. Even though both the victim and her older sister agreed that the burn was accidental, I was convinced that the older sister held the curling iron on her sister's arm intentionally. The burn was deep, and I didn't think an accidental burn could be that profound. My fixation was in part because I wanted to cover my bases. I didn't want to be like the social worker who let the abusive mother off. A detective worked the case with me. He felt assured that the burn was accidental, but I wouldn't let it go. To satisfy me, the detective sent the medical report to a medical examiner in Georgia who agreed that the wound was consistent with an accidental burn from a curling iron. I was wrong.

Agencies can compensate for one professional getting something wrong by having other professionals on the case get it right. If the police officer shows an error in judgment, the case could be rectified if the social worker points out what the officer missed; the district attorney reviews the entire file (including recordings) and asks that additional leads be pursued; the doctor refuses to agree with the police officer's theory because it doesn't match the injury; or other police officers working on the case challenge its direction. The various agencies involved can act as a safety net when one car in the train goes off the tracks. But when everybody on the case feeds off each other to reinforce the theory they've already decided is true, the result can be a preverbal child being sent back to her house where her injury occurred, while the wrong caregiver is accused of the crime.

❧

I spent two months writing my report to DCF. I was still at home with the kids, so I worked on the letter in whatever free time I could scrounge up. I could never devote entire days to writing and that, coupled with the amount of information I had to sift through, meant that this project spanned more than just a few days. Although I sometimes felt resentment for having to spend my spare moments writing about this nonsense, I had so many things I wanted to say that I became a little obsessive about it. Even when I wasn't actively working on the letter, I was thinking about what I should write in the letter. As I was preparing dinner, I was thinking about what I wanted to say and how I wanted to say it. I was chopping the veggies, stirring the sauce, searing the steaks, and writing the letter in my mind.

Writing this particular letter was hard. I had a massive volume of information to weed through and organize. In addition to not being allowed to have physical copies of any documents, I also wasn't allowed to type up a transcript of the recordings. All I had of the case file were pictures on my phone of the reports from the computer screen and notes from the recordings I had written in a notebook. When I picked a topic to write about, I had to flip back through my notebooks and swipe through my phone to find the relevant statements. It was painstaking and overwhelming.

I vacillated between feeling confident that telling people what happened was the right thing to do and thinking that I should accept what happened to me and move on. I often wondered if what I was trying to accomplish was a complete waste of my time. Who was going to listen to me and, if they did listen, who was going to care?

There were times when I doubted myself. I would stop and ask, *Am I getting this right? Did she actually say that? Did he really not write that down?* The investigation and the reports were so bad that sometimes I thought it had to be my mistake for thinking they were that bad because nothing could be that bad. I wondered if I was imagining things, but it was there in print and on recording.

During the active investigation, I let fear guide me. I didn't listen to that little voice in my head screaming at me to protect myself because something wasn't right. I ignored all signs that told me not to talk to Daniel Holland about the hug and to decline the polygraph. I had learned my lesson, and by now I was committed to doing things differently. Instead of leading with panic and hysteria, I chose to slow down, listen to my inner guidance, pray continually, and trust myself. I invoked the name of every angel and saint I knew to help me write, including hanging a picture of Uriel, archangel of wisdom, on the wall directly across from my writing space.

I wanted to finish the report, but I also wanted to take my time to get it right. There were times when I felt it was taking way too long, but my slowed pace had its benefits. Help came to me in forms I didn't anticipate. What are the odds that while I was arguing that Abigail was capable of playing the bongo drums with a broken arm, my own child's broken arm would go undetected for two weeks? Or that Kelly Anderson would walk into Mike's office and we would find out she was friends with Daniel Holland? I did not foresee those scenarios, but I was more than willing to use them to my advantage.

Bailey's letter totaled eight pages. By the time I finished comparing the reports with the recordings, addressing the way DCF responded to Bailey, and explaining it in exhaustive detail so that nobody would miss what I was saying, my letter was fifty-seven pages long. When I hit page twenty, I started calling it a report. I thought it deserved at least that much.

At the end of my report, I requested that DCF overturn my finding, communicate to the Holders exactly what happened with the investigation, reimburse me for the seven thousand dollars I paid to my lawyer, audit all of Hannah Taylor's recent findings, and review any appeals processed by Teresa Walker. I asked for a copy of my report to be included in the file of every DCF employee who worked on my case. Lastly, I wrote, "I would feel much better if I knew that the individuals reading this letter took it to heart and made a commitment to understanding what went wrong in this case so it can be avoided on other cases."

In addition to sending a copy of my report to the DCF Secretary, I also sent a copy to the DCF legal department and two other high-ranking DCF employees that worked in DCF's central office. I was initially going to send copies to Hannah Taylor, Kelly Anderson, and Teresa Walker but decided against it. I thought there was a possibility that upper management might want to ask them about their role in what occurred, and I considered that it might be beneficial if they weren't notified of the contents of the report first.

I sent a copy to Dr. Mitchell, her supervisor, and the director of their unit. I hoped Dr. Mitchell might be inclined to change her mind after she learned all the facts. If Dr. Mitchell agreed that Abigail's behavior indicated her injury happened before she arrived at my house, I would be exonerated. DCF would have a much harder time blaming me for Abigail's injury without a doctor's supporting statement.

I considered sending my report to the director of the KBI and the Kansas attorney general but decided against it. I was still within the statute of limitations, and Holland and the attorney general's office were the two entities that could work to bring charges against me. The limited information available about the attorney general's work on my case did nothing to assure me that my case would be handled fairly.

On June 29, 2015, when the DA decided not to press charges, Assistant Attorney General Lisa Stuart penned a letter that said, in part, "After a review of all of the available evidence and consultation with the parents of Abigail Holder, it is our decision to decline to file charges in this matter." The phrase "consultation with the parents of Abigail Holder" is key in that statement because I believe had Meredith and Steve pressed hard for charges, the outcome could have been different.

I don't know what Lisa Stuart was referring to when she referenced "all of the available evidence." I don't know if she listened to the recordings or just went off the reports, but what is obvious is that a lawyer at the Kansas attorney general's office called the most likely suspect (Steve Holder) and asked him if he wanted charges pressed against an innocent person. Thankfully he had the decency to say no. I'm actually hopeful that she didn't listen to the recordings, because if she did so and still consulted with Steve and Meredith to discuss charging me, then that would lead me to question her ability to adequately analyze information on child abuse cases. Either way, I didn't want to provoke her with my letter while I could still be charged with the crime.

In addition to making copies of my report, I copied my relevant medical records that discussed the condition of my hands, Meredith's email to Holland, and my attorney's letter. I also included several pictures: a picture of me to show my stature, a picture of my swollen hands, a picture of Abigail in down dog to show that you couldn't see her face and therefore didn't know she was whining, and a picture of Daniel Holland's Facebook profile picture with Kelly Anderson's picture in the bottom corner that proved they were friends.

While waiting in line at the post office with my big stack of manila envelopes, I glanced at a container full of greeting cards on the counter. The stack of cards in the middle partition were partially obscured by the ones in front, but clearly visible was one word: *Courage*.

Chapter 18

The Response

THE WORST SITUATIONS I ever found myself in at DCF were when I was forced to remove an infant from a mother at the hospital right after she had given birth. This didn't happen often, but when it did, I always felt like a monster, even when it was justified. A very young mom gave birth to a baby fathered by a man who had a savage history, leaving me with no choice but to place the newborn boy in foster care for his own safety. While the mom was still in her hospital bed, I arrived in her room and explained that I had a judge's order for removal of her baby from her care. She was young and had been battered by life's storms, but she looked at me with fire in her eyes and said, "You're not taking my baby." I said, "Yes I am." And I did.

Two days later, as I drove down the road to the hearing on her case, I passed the mother walking—*walking*—to the courthouse, roughly a mile from her house, a mere forty-eight hours after giving birth. The sight of her hit me like a punch in the gut. I almost pulled over to ask her if she wanted a ride, but thought better of it. I was probably the last person on the face of the earth that she wanted to see or be stuck in a car with. I still don't know if that was the right or the wrong decision.

At the hearing I learned that the foster care contractor had declined to give the mother a ride to the courthouse for the hearing—*forty-eight hours after she gave birth to a human being*—because it was against protocol to drive parents to their first court hearing. They had an opportunity to act humanely and respond in a sensible way to someone's suffering, and they came back with, "Well, you see, we have this protocol. . . ."

⚬

After mailing my report, I went on with summer plans and waited to see what would happen. We went on vacation to Florida, played T-ball, and made our daily trips to the pool or lake for swimming. I knew better than to be waiting on the edge of my seat.

My response from DCF arrived on July 13, 2017. It was not written by anybody I mailed my letter to, but was instead a single page from the director of client services that read,

> DCF administrative staff has reviewed your letter and the accompanying documentation you provided. The requests that you made of DCF, at the conclusion of your letter, were also considered. You also acknowledged in your letter that you withdrew your appeal of the finding and did not complete the appellate process afforded to you by law. It is the position of DCF that it would not be appropriate to make determinations regarding this matter outside of the official standard appeal process. DCF supports the substantiated finding based on information disclosed in the investigative report, which has not been reversed or altered as the result of an appeal.

DCF had an easy way out of this mess: listen to a few recordings, blame the whole thing on Daniel Holland, backtrack their finding, and apologize for the pain caused. Instead they fell back on policy and protocol.

This was doubly frustrating because DCF went against their own policy several times on this case. It is not DCF policy for a supervisor to leave a case file on a shelf for a year, but Hannah Taylor did that. It is not DCF policy to substantiate someone for hugging a child when their own medical expert says hugging a child can't cause a spiral fracture, but DCF staff did that. It is not DCF policy for a supervisor to withhold information from a doctor to influence the doctor's medical opinion, but Hannah Taylor did that. I sent them my report detailing the scandalous behavior of their staff, and then they were concerned with how things are supposed to be done.

I know from working there that DCF can do anything they want to do, regardless of policy. They could have overturned my finding if they wanted to, but they didn't. I suspect that DCF refused to take me off the Child Abuse Registry because of the risk of a lawsuit and terrible publicity. What happened to me is bad, but what could have happened to Abigail when she was returned to her home is the real problem. You can't read my report and not understand that. Failures like this can easily result in a child's death.

I provided DCF with a moral dilemma and they responded with a legal answer that completely ignored the central issue—the safety of a young child. When you are the state child welfare agency, you can't say it would be "inappropriate" for you to do something about a child's welfare because *doing something about it is your job*.

Investigators from all agencies missed an opportunity to hold the real perpetrator accountable, but they also missed an opportunity to do something far more important: provide assistance to the Holder family. DCF missed the chance to support a family during a painful period and help them remedy what went wrong. Healing is the whole point.

The date on DCF's response to my report was July 11, 2017.

Just a few weeks later, on August 4, 2017, the DCF Secretary published an open letter in the *Lawrence Journal-World* newspaper in response to reports of questionable behavior by DCF. She wrote, "And as an agency, we are constantly striving to identify innovative and tested successful strategies to improve the well-being of children in our state. Our interest is particularly for those who cannot protect themselves from the abuse and neglect they suffer at the hands of their caregivers or others."2

The Secretary didn't clarify whether one of those innovative strategies was to conduct a timely and thorough investigation to identify the correct perpetrator so that the child isn't left in the residence where the injury occurred with no determination of her safety. She also didn't clarify if by "others" she meant her own staff.

❧

The first step in fixing something is to acknowledge what is broken. Moving forward is almost impossible otherwise. But we also need to consider how we, as a society, respond to an admission of failure. People and agencies are less inclined to admit wrongdoing if they think they will be persecuted for it and, in turn, society is less inclined to offer mercy to an agency that seems to never admit when it's wrong. Accountability can be a vicious cycle.

I'm upset that DCF swept my case under the rug, but I also understand why they tried it as an initial strategy. I've been on both sides. With Abigail's case, I was a direct recipient of DCF's bullying, incompetence, failure to admit wrongdoing, tone-deaf response to complaints, and refusal to fix mistakes. I'm *real clear* on how they operate. But during my ten years as a CPS worker, I had a front-row seat to being blamed for every bad thing that happened, even things beyond my control.

2 Gilmore, Phyllis. 2017, August 4. *Your turn: DCF Secretary elaborates on task force goals.* Lawrence Journal World. *https://www2.ljworld.com/news/2017/aug/04/your-turn-dcf-secretary-elaborates-task-force-goal/*

Something that became apparent to me early in my career is that whatever I did, someone was unhappy about it. Even if a problem wasn't my fault, somebody would blame me anyway.

Our decision-making was constantly critiqued, and any mistakes were pounced on. We got it from all sides—parents, community partners, judges, lawyers. I sometimes left the courtroom wondering if excoriating a social worker on the stand is the equivalent of an Olympic event for attorneys. Stories always circulated of workers breaking down in tears in court.

I worked each case so that the child would be safe. I also worked each case so that *I* would be safe, because I knew if the client made a bad choice on my watch, I could be skewered for it. I cared what happened to the family, of course, but I also cared about what might happen to me if I couldn't prove that I had done my job. I wanted my documentation to be in order so if a client made a mistake I could say, "This isn't my fault because I told them not to do that."

I once tagged along on a home visit with a social worker named Natalie. The mother was facing allegation of failure to thrive for her young baby. Natalie's most recent contact with the child was the previous week, when the baby seemed small but not obviously malnourished. Now, after receiving additional information, Natalie was going back out for another visit. On the day I went with Natalie, the baby's face seemed round and filled out, but when her mother undressed her at Natalie's request, it became alarmingly clear that she was starving. Natalie moved to get the child immediate medical treatment and involved the court system. The mother was not acting out of malice, but the child's physical condition was concerning enough to merit court oversight. I attended the subsequent court hearing and watched as the attorneys grilled Natalie about the actions she took on the case, why she didn't visit the child for a week, and why she didn't prevent the child from almost starving to death. The attorneys nearly spent more time attempting to make Natalie responsible for the child almost dying than the child's parents.

I wanted to raise my hand and ask, Do you understand that Natalie is not the child's parent? That Natalie herself was not failing to breastfeed the child? Natalie did the best she could. When notified of the situation, she responded immediately. The parents are ultimately responsible for this child's condition, not Natalie.

Compounding my frustration was the fact that I knew Natalie was a great social worker and was suffering terrible emotional distress over the child's condition. This wasn't my case, and even I couldn't shake the image of the child's emaciated little body. The attorneys didn't need to pile on, because Natalie was already painfully aware of what had happened. But do you know what Natalie would have been accused of if she had checked on the child every day? Harassment.

Being a good social worker takes time, practice, and experience. Even at their very best, social workers will never be able to prevent every bad thing from happening to a child. If a state agency is held to that outrageous standard, they will always fail.

Being responsible for others' behavior in addition to your own can be difficult, especially when those other people struggle with mental health disorders and drug problems. Dysfunctional things happen when you deal with dysfunctional people. I was expected to help people redeem themselves, but I was also expected to predict the future and know when redemption wasn't going to happen. How was I supposed to know who was a one-time offender and who was going to continue hurting their child? I didn't have a crystal ball. I could only respond the best way I knew how in the moment, and sometimes my best wasn't good enough. Some of the families I worked with had been dysfunctional for decades—sometimes going back before I was born—and I didn't want to be responsible for not being able to fix them.

In the tragic event when a child dies, DCF gets slammed for

not doing enough. When DCF does too much to make sure a child doesn't die, they get persecuted for that too. When workers feel like they can't win no matter what, sometimes they stop trying to win. Sometimes DCF will get things wrong when they shouldn't have, and that's what happened on my case. And sometimes DCF gets it wrong when they had no chance of ever getting it right. Laying every misfortune on their doorstep is not only unfair, it's also ineffective. When we try to blame DCF for *everything*, they swing the other way and accept responsibility for *nothing*. Or they just hope nobody finds out about it at all.

I want my former agency to be successful because I know how hard it is to be a social worker in Child Protective Services. I enjoyed my work and would likely still be working there today if the high cost of childcare and my small paycheck hadn't made my career impossible to continue. The work continues to be valuable and necessary, and I want DCF to be good at it. When they make mistakes, I want them to acknowledge that and work to fix it. Imagine what we could do if DCF held themselves accountable, and the public responded with grace, helpfulness, and thoughtful solutions.

✍

I wasn't the only one having trouble with DCF. Recent press coverage of the agency was dominating headlines.

In spring of 2017, around the time I sent my report to DCF, journalists wrote about a seven-year-old boy named Adrian Jones who was tortured by his father and stepmother in Kansas City, Kansas, and, when he died of starvation in 2015, his corpse was fed to pigs on their farm. A secondary thread ran through reports on his case: how DCF responded to repeated hotline calls and the fact that Adrian was left at home with his parents, where he later died.

On November 20, 2017, Shannon O'Brien and Lisa McCormick, writing for Fox 4 News in Kansas City, quoted

Diane Keech, former deputy director at DCF, "Keech said Adrian was not just a child who fell through the cracks, and it wasn't just one incident led to him being fed to the pigs—but rather every single case was mishandled."3

The bad press didn't stop with Adrian Jones. On November 12, 2017, Laura Bauer wrote in the *Kansas City Star*: "Clint Blansett's 10-year-old son had been dead just a few days when a social worker from the state knocked on the family's door in south-central Kansas. She wasn't there to offer condolences after Caleb's death or ask about his sister, Blansett said. She wanted him to sign a form saying he wouldn't talk about his son's death or the Kansas Department for Children and Families. No details about contact the agency had with the family before Caleb's mom smashed his head with a rock while he slept and then stabbed him seven times."

Later in the article, Laura Bauer continued, "What Caleb's father faced that day in December 2014 is what other parents and Kansas legislators say they've battled for years: An agency charged with protecting kids instead focused on protecting itself. An agency where a former high-level DCF supervisor told the *Star* she was instructed not to document anything after a child's death and to shred notes after meetings so attorneys and reporters couldn't get them through open records requests. An agency where even lawmakers insist DCF officials are intentionally misleading them and providing information the Legislature can't trust."4

3 O'Brien, Shannon and McCormick, Lisa. (2017, November 20). FOX 4 investigation finds systemic failures at Kansas DCF that allowed Adrian Jones' torture to continue. *Fox 4 Problem Solvers*. https://fox4kc.com/news/problem-solvers/fox-4-investigation-finds-systemic-failures-at-kansas-dcf-that-allowed-adrian-jones-torture-to-continue/

4 Bauer, Laura. (2017, November 12). Secrecy inside child welfare system can kill: 'God help the children of Kansas.' *Kansas City Star*. https://www.kansascity.com/news/politics-government/article184177786.html

I was confused when I read about the shredding of documents. When I worked there, we were repeatedly admonished to document everything on a case. The higher the profile of the case, the more we were told to document our conversations. I went so far as to record conversations on big cases so I could transcribe exactly what was said. If I approached one of my supervisors about a case that had problems, inevitably their response would include two words: *Log it*. If I had shredded a document, I would have faced serious consequences.

The articles confused me, but they also made me a little sad. I had only been gone six years, but it seemed like my previous employer had done a one-eighty. What happened?

In response to growing concerns about how DCF was handling its business, Kansas lawmakers put together a task force of community members, some of whom were legislators. The job of the task force was to assess the system and provide recommendations, with a focus on the foster care component of the child welfare system. Foster care is important, obviously, but the dysfunction within child welfare goes well beyond just that one part. Adrian Jones wasn't in foster care, and neither was Abigail. If you want to fix child welfare, including foster care, you need to start at the beginning.

Even though their focus was on foster care, I thought the task force might be interested in my story as it related to DCF's general functioning. I read newspaper reports and picked task force members who seemed to have the most constructive things to say. I wrote a lengthy cover letter explaining the case, including my substantiation, my appeal, the comparison of the recordings with the written documents, and DCF's response to my report. I explained that I wasn't asking legislators to involve themselves in my case but wanted to offer them my story to factor into their recommendations. I made more copies of my report at Kinko's and put together more packets.

The DCF Secretary retired effective December 1, 2017, and Stephanie Martin became the new secretary. Stephanie Martin had worked in the child welfare system for decades for different agencies, and I knew her from my time at DCF. I wasn't friends with her, but I knew her well enough to say hello when I saw her. I put together a packet for Stephanie because I believed she should know what had recently happened within the agency she was about to be the leader of.

I never received any correspondence from anyone on the task force or Stephanie. I heard through the grapevine that Stephanie was "really upset" by the contents of my report and had assigned an "independent group" to look into it. I was never formally notified about the group or what they uncovered, but I was eventually told by an insider that sixteen people listened to the recordings and reviewed the reports and "everybody knows it was wrong." But the people who knew I was on the Registry for something I didn't do while Abigail was returned to her home still did nothing to remedy the situation.

After I received DCF's response, I was out of options. I could appeal to no one else besides the newspaper, and I wasn't interested in going that route. Everyone's seeming uninterest in my report made me question my entire experience. Maybe returning a preverbal child to her residence where the abuse occurred didn't really matter. Maybe the wrong caregiver being accused of the crime while the actual perpetrator hangs out with the child at home is nothing to get worked up about. Maybe a cop writing misleading police reports and a doctor making stuff up is trivial. Maybe the only reason why I thought it was a big deal was because it happened to me.

I understand that moral outrage gets old and self-righteous indignation grows tiresome. We can't care about *everything*—but I felt that we should care about *this*. I didn't necessarily expect anybody to care about me, but I found it a little appalling that nobody seemed to care that much about Abigail. Given the mistakes that DCF appeared to be making around this time, I thought someone would be concerned about Abigail and want to fix what went wrong so it didn't happen to someone else.

Chapter 19

The Big Picture

THIS STORY IS believable, even in all its absurdity. Why wouldn't you believe it? Beyond the fact that I used reports from Children's Mercy Hospital, the KBI, and DCF to prove my claims, the story I'm telling you is believable because *I'm* believable. I check all of the privilege boxes—I'm white, middle-class, articulate, educated—but the things that really set me apart and increase my credibility are that I'm a former CPS social worker and I'm married to a police officer. When someone who is a part of the system uses insider information to criticize the system, people pay attention.

But what if this same exact scenario happened to someone very different? Imagine you are standing in front of a woman in her trailer that smells like cat urine with her five dirty kids, all of whom have different fathers. She's missing teeth and misuses adjectives. You see cigarette butts in the ashtray and cockroaches on the wall, and you ask her why she's on the Child Abuse Registry. She answers, "The lead investigator on the case didn't ask the right questions to the right people and omitted most of the relevant facts in his reports. The doctor from the best children's hospital made up how I caused the injury and everybody believed her. DCF substantiated me for something their own medical expert said couldn't have caused a spiral fracture and, when I appealed it, DCF didn't give the doctor all the available information so that they could win the appeal."

Would you believe her? Probably not. The story sounds unbelievable when an uneducated woman in a trailer is telling it, because how could a woman like that be right and all the professionals be wrong? Nobody is going to believe someone like her over a police officer or a social worker or a doctor. *Nobody.* The woman I have described for you is fictitious, but walk into any courtroom or DCF lobby in America and you'll see women just like her.

I have the work experience, life experience, and education necessary to look at my case objectively and write a coherent narrative about what happened that will make sense to people who are willing to listen. I know how to form a logical argument using an investigator's own data because I used to be an investigator. How do disadvantaged people fight back? What do you do—and how frustrated do you feel—when the professionals say the wrong things about you and you can't convince anyone otherwise? Defending yourself against the system—any system—costs time and money. Even though I had the time, a little bit of money, and the truth on my side, I still couldn't win. Fighting the child welfare system was so hard, so overwhelming, and so frustrating that eventually even I gave up and dropped my appeal.

I don't think one bad investigation by one officer means that all police officers are bad. That's silly. However, it's unrealistic to think that Holland's actions wouldn't alter my views on law enforcement in general. Do you blame me? How do I know the next officer I run into isn't going to do the same thing Holland did? I don't, and so I'm going to be on guard against all officers until they show me that I can trust them. This was my first and only time being investigated for a crime. It took one investigation for me to be skeptical of the police as an institution, and *I'm married to a police officer.*

I believe that the vast majority of officers are trying to do the right thing. I also understand that some of them aren't, at least not all the time, and you can't tell the difference just by looking at them. You might get a good officer or you might get one who almost wrecks your life, and you're not going to know which one you got until it's too late. It's easy to take the actions of a few and generalize them to the whole, and so who else becomes suspect when Daniel Holland acts like this? My husband, my brother-in-law, and all the other cops who are trying to do good in the world. Being a police officer is hard enough. Daniel Holland not only disrespected me with his poor work product but he also insulted every good cop out there.

❧

Some years after I was investigated, one of my friends happened to be at a training with Dr. Mitchell. I asked her for a physical description of Dr. Mitchell—since I had never actually met her—and my friend texted, *She's beautiful, trendy, and well-spoken.*

I texted back, *She may be all of those things, but she still messed up when she guessed wrong. You put someone like her up against an addict in a trailer park and that guy's going to jail even if she's wrong. That's what I'm trying to tell people.*

Before I was investigated, whenever I followed a criminal trial in the news, I assumed that the medical experts working for the prosecution were unbiased and concerned only with the truth, while the medical experts hired by the defense would provide whatever testimony was necessary for acquittal, even if it wasn't true. Had my case gone to trial, Dr. Desiree Mitchell—who guessed, incorrectly, that Abigail wouldn't have been able to play the bongo drums with a broken arm and who made up a story about me that had no basis in fact—wouldn't have been a defense witness. She would have been a prosecution witness.

Medical opinions play a vital role in substantiating findings and charging people with crimes. If you can get a doctor to agree with your theory, you're on your way to a substantiation or a conviction. If you can get a doctor to say it happened, then it happened. If you can't get a doctor's opinion that supports your theory, you're stuck. This principle also works in reverse. Police officers and social workers don't have medical degrees, and so they rely on doctors to explain injuries to them. But if the doctor is wrong about how an injury could have occurred, the police officer then conducts an investigation—including interrogating suspects—with the wrong information. Examining DCF and the police is crucial, but just as important is understanding how medical professionals contribute. DCF wouldn't have been able to get away with what they did if it weren't for Dr. Mitchell.

Children's Mercy Hospital, where Dr. Mitchell worked during this investigation, has a reputation for being the best of the best when it comes to treating children. Dr. Mitchell worked in the SCAN program, part of the Division of Child Adversity and Resilience at Children's Mercy Hospital. According to their website, "each year we work with nearly 3,000 children by identifying, preventing, and treating all forms of child abuse."5 At the time of my investigation, Dr. Mitchell was the associate program director of the pediatric residency program and an associate professor of pediatrics at a local college. Dr. Mitchell is not some quack with an online medical degree who runs a seedy medical practice out of a strip mall. She's one of the best. And because she's one of the

---

5   https://www.childrensmercy.org/departments-and-clinics/
child-adversity-and-resilience/safety-care-and-nurturing/

best, people who sit on juries are inclined to believe her, even when she's wrong. On my case, she was wrong. Yes, this affected me directly, but more importantly, Dr. Mitchell's opinion was potentially disastrous for Abigail. Even smart people who wear nice clothes are wrong sometimes.

Dr. Mitchell didn't give an opinion just based on what is medically possible. She gave an opinion based, in part, on the information she received from Daniel Holland. Per DCF log notes, she requested DCF reports and police reports to finish her own assessment because she didn't have "any documentation of any trauma history or explanation for the fracture." Dr. Mitchell was looking for context from investigators to give her opinion on what happened. One problem with that approach is that the person providing the context was Daniel Holland, and the context he provided was wrong. A second problem is that by focusing on context, Dr. Mitchell concerned herself with things that were outside the scope of her job.

Whether it happens formally or informally, child abuse investigations are conducted by interdisciplinary teams where each member plays a specific role. The doctor uses medical knowledge to determine how injuries occur and if they are consistent with the explanation given. Police officers determine if a crime occurred and arrest perpetrators. Social workers figure out if the child is safe and, if not, what services are needed. This approach is great when everybody stays in their lane, but it can be a disaster when somebody goes out of bounds. Dr. Mitchell was in the role of doctor but took it upon herself to play the role of police officer as well, and, in doing so, she is just as responsible as Holland for keeping Abigail in potential danger.

When Dr. Mitchell started writing about my state of mind, how I felt about breaking Abigail's arm, and her definitive statement that I caused the injury, she took on the role of investigator. All those details—the *who, what, when* and *why*—was Holland's job. Dr. Mitchell's only job was the *how*. She should have given an opinion based on the mechanics of the injury and left it at that.

Dr. Mitchell delved into the areas of context and intent—which is the role of law enforcement and, beyond that, the district attorney's office. When Dr. Mitchell played police officer, she enabled Holland and DCF to say, "We have a doctor saying that Andrea caused the injury," which is all they needed to proceed with their case against me

When I was employed, I don't remember ever questioning a medical diagnosis or opinion coming out of Children's Mercy Hospital. I was always extremely grateful that we were so close to their SCAN team. Hard cases of child abuse were routinely sent there because we wanted the best medical opinion we could get on a case and we thought we were getting that from Children's Mercy. Maybe we were, but maybe we weren't. How could we ever know?

∽

The professionals in child welfare don't come with a warning label. When a cop walks in the interview room, he doesn't say, "Hello, I'm the officer assigned to your case and there have been multiple occasions when I have been grossly incompetent." When a doctor discusses your diagnosis with you, she doesn't say, "I want to warn you that I tend to make stuff up. I'm probably right about 75 percent of the time." I have never known a social worker to say to a client, "I substantiate people for things I can't prove they did just because I can."

After being investigated, the people I lost faith in were the professionals. I didn't become critical of welfare recipients, drug addicts, felons, people of color, or the mentally ill. The people who made me mistrustful were cops, social workers, and a doctor.

Chapter 20

The Aftermath, Part II

ABOUT A YEAR and a half after the active investigation, I took the twins to a park to play on a nice afternoon. Shortly after we arrived, Steve and Abigail walked over to play without knowing that we were already there. The park was small, and we couldn't exactly avoid each other, so Steve and I stood there awkwardly while the kids played on the same equipment. I didn't have time to feel any anger towards him because I was distracted by a tidal wave of sadness. As our kids ran around, I realized that they didn't remember each other at all. My boys had enjoyed helping take care of Abigail and they'd had so many adventures together, but now they were at a park with no idea how their lives had been previously intertwined. Our kids were collateral damage in this botched investigation.

❧

Steve and Meredith were front and center in my mind during 2017 when I battled DCF, but outside of the high school graduation of our children, I didn't cross paths with them very often. Two days after receiving DCF's response to my report, I walked into the public swimming pool and saw Meredith, who I had never seen at the pool before, sitting on a lawn chair. Faced with the prospect of—once again!—being in her presence while remaining silent and acting like her family hadn't hijacked my life, I looked at her and thought, *Not today*. Adopting a commanding presence in a swimsuit isn't easy, but I made a mental note to flex my abs extra hard, and after spraying Thomas and Joseph with sunscreen and sending them on their way, I sat down next to Meredith on an empty chair.

Never one to beat around the bush, I started by saying, "Hi, Meredith. I want you to know I didn't break Abigail's arm. I only thought I did because it never occurred to me that someone at your house would break her arm and let me take the blame for it."

She waved her hand like she was shooing away a fly and said, "Oh . . . no . . . " as if she were dismissing the notion that someone in her family would do that.

I continued, "I've read all the documents and it's obvious that she was injured when she arrived."

Meredith replied, "She was fine when she was dropped off," confirming my suspicions that she bought into Steve's lie that Abigail was uninjured that morning.

"Actually, she wasn't. She was in a mood when she was dropped off. I just didn't think anything of it."

Meredith replied, "I'm just trying to move past it and move on."

You would like to move on? YOU would like to move on? I said, "It's hard for me to move on because I'm on the Child Abuse Registry for something I didn't do. The investigation was a joke. DCF has acted very poorly. Hugging a child is not abusive and can't cause a spiral fracture anyway because there has to be twisting."

Meredith nodded in the affirmative, and I noted that Abigail was starting to make her way back to their chair. While I had lowered my standards enough to discuss a felony matter at a public swimming pool while wearing a bikini, I wasn't willing to continue the conversation in front of a child. As I got up to leave, I said, "Well, I just wanted to make sure you know I didn't break her arm. I hope your family is doing well." They stayed at the pool and so did I, but we didn't interact anymore outside of this.

I didn't get to say everything I wanted to say to Meredith. I likely never will but, on this day at least, I took back a little of my power that had been held hostage for years.

⌘

In December of 2018—the same month that the statute of limitations expired—my son Ryan wrecked Jared Holder's vehicle. It looked like we were never going to get away from the Holder family. Mike had to speak with Steve several times about insurance issues and payment to have the car replaced. During one phone conversation with Steve, Mike said, "Speaking of personal responsibility, there's something I've wanted to talk to you about for five years." Mike told Steve straight up that we believed he had broken Abigail's arm, dropped her off with me, and let me take the blame.

Mike went after Steve for almost an hour, and Steve sat there and took it, his only response being, "It was so long ago that I don't remember." In what seemed like an attempt to absolve himself, Steve explained that Holland and "a lady" came to his house and tried to get him to agree to having charges filed against me, which Steve declined.

On January 2, 2019, I sent Meredith a private message on Facebook Messenger because I didn't have her current phone number. I explained that the statute of limitations had ended, and I wanted to speak with her to explain my side of the story. Facebook Messenger alerted me that Meredith read my message, but she never responded.

Over the next several weeks, Mike and Steve continued to communicate about the wrecked car. Steve expressed that he wanted the car replaced as soon as possible. Insurance totaled Jared's car at $3,700 and paid $2,700 of that amount, and Mike and I were responsible for the remaining $1,000. Without hesitation, I wrote Steve Holder a check for $1,000. I never considered not writing that check.

Mike and I have joint accounts, and I told Mike that I would be the one to write and sign the check. Along with it, I wrote a one-page letter to Steve. I outlined my theory that he was responsible, called him out for lying to Daniel Holland, and told him he was lucky that Holland and Lockhart were the investigating officers, because someone with more sense would have figured it out. I listed the ways in which his actions affected me, including the limits it placed on my employment options and my inability to volunteer at my children's school. The last item on the list was, *I have spent over $10,000 on legal fees and other expenses defending myself against something that occurred at your residence before you dropped Abigail off at my house.* Directly after that I started a new paragraph: *Enclosed is a $1,000 check for the portion of the car that insurance doesn't cover. Mike and I believe in taking care of what is ours. It's never too late to do the right thing.* With no anxiety or fanfare, I signed it and put it in the mail.

Steve and Meredith didn't respond to me, but Steve never did cash that check. His decision not to do so is likely the closest thing to an apology I'm ever going to get.

Chapter 21

The Crusade

THE CHILD WELFARE system is the last line of defense for abused children and families, so what do you do when the system is the problem? Who do you appeal to when the people charged with fixing the situation are the ones who caused it?

By this time, I was as worn out living this experience as you might be reading about it. I continued to be concerned about how this case impacted my own life and my ability to find employment. But I am also a social worker deep down in my heart, and I couldn't shake the conviction that this story mattered. If I could just find the right person to tell it to, then we could do better for other people. I had notified two different DCF directors, Dr. Mitchell and her supervisor, and a task force, and had been soundly rejected every time. But how do you give up when you know how much is at stake?

When my statute of limitations ran out on December 2, 2018—five frustrating, defeating years after this whole thing started—I was able to say whatever I wanted to whomever I wanted to say it.

Without any hand-wringing, I made the decision to hop in

my minivan and drive around northeastern Kansas calling out everybody I knew to be wrong. I compiled a list of agencies I wanted to speak the truth to and aimed to shoot for the highest representative I could reach. My plan was to not only give them a copy of my report, but to also provide a cover letter that clearly summarized how their agency failed.

You can talk all day long, but you can't make people listen.

∽

Mike and I first met with the Police Chief at the Eudora Police Department. He was not the chief when the investigation was ongoing, but he agreed to meet anyway.

I explained everything from start to finish. The Chief asked clarifying questions, but he mostly just listened. When I finished, he said, "I can see how you would be disappointed in what happened."

It was the first—and only—time any agency representative had acknowledged my feelings or frustration.

∽

Mike obtained a KBI contact through one of his friends, and we arranged to meet with agent Jeff Turner in the Professional Standards Department at the KBI facility in Topeka, Kansas. I was prepared to briefly discuss the contents of my cover letter, but Jeff Turner turned it into a three-hour interview. I found it easy to talk, because all I had to do was tell the truth.

After our initial meeting, Turner interviewed Steve and Meredith (which yielded no confession) and presented the omitted information to Dr. Mitchell (which did not result in her changing her mind). I appreciated his effort and I have respect for how hard he tried to make things right, but Turner was never going to be able to fix what Holland broke. Later in a follow-up phone call, Turner made two noteworthy statements that he would later repeat to Mike: First, he had listened to the recordings and couldn't tell who injured Abigail. Second, what I said about Daniel Holland's behavior was accurate.

The letter from the KBI director arrived a couple months later:

> "Based upon the results of the investigation, I have concluded that there is no clear evidence to support the assertion contained in the complaint and no further action will be taken by the KBI."

I did not expect—or want—Holland to be fed to the wolves. Still, I felt his actions merited an acknowledgment by KBI management. Even a generic statement that Holland's work didn't meet the KBI's standards would have been well-received by me. I'm obviously concerned that Holland wrote his reports in the way that he did, but it's also troubling that he thought he could get away with it. But then again, he did what he did with zero external consequences. Maybe he always knew he wouldn't have to answer for his actions.

⤚⟍

I couldn't locate a way to file a complaint on the attorney general's website and so I sent an email to the *Contact Us* email listed on their website. I didn't know who was going to read it, so I stayed general:

> I am writing regarding an investigation against me in 2013–2014 that was forwarded to the attorney general's office and reviewed by Lisa Stuart. I gained access to the investigative file (including recordings and police reports) through the DCF appeal process. The officer conducted a very poor investigation and then misrepresented information and/or lied in his police reports. This resulted

in a small child continuing to reside in her home where the abuse occurred without safety intervention. I would like to speak with someone in your office about this as the officer is still employed, and I feel that I have a moral obligation to alert agencies who were involved in the case.

This was the response I received:

Please be aware that under Kansas law, this office does not control the various activities of municipal police departments. Each law enforcement agency is subject to the direction of the chief of police who is usually appointed by the local municipal elected governing body. We suggest that you make the chief of police where the incident occurred aware of your concerns. We trust this information is useful to you. Please contact our office again if we can assist you with future matters within our jurisdiction.

The following statement is clearly visible on the KBI's website: "The KBI is a division of the Office of Attorney General and is led by a director appointed by the attorney general." I emailed back to clarify:

Thank you for your response to my email. I have already spoken with the chief of police where I live as he graciously agreed to meet with me to hear what I have to say.

My case was not forwarded to the Douglas County District Attorney's Office because my husband is a detective in the Lawrence Kansas Police Department. It was forwarded to your office, as I stated in my initial email. That's why I contacted you. Additionally, the officer involved works for the KBI, which adds to its relevance to your agency.

I want to meet with a representative of your office to explain what the KBI did on my case. It involves leaving a preverbal child at her residence where her injury occurred while the agent focused exclusively on me, and then he misrepresented and/or lied in his reports that he turned in to the Attorney General's Office. An assistant AG reviewed his reports, which is why I want to meet with a representative of your agency.

My intent is not to complain for the sake of complaining. My intent is to make everybody aware of what happened on my case in the hopes that better choices will be made in the future. When the system fails, the people who suffer are vulnerable children.

I sincerely hope that this additional information will change your mind and you will agree to arrange a meeting. If you are declining to meet with me, please email me back to state that.

I never received a response to my email, and I never met with anyone from the Kansas attorney general's office.

I called the Children's Mercy Hospital Risk Management Department and spoke to Monica. I began, "I was investigated for child abuse on a case that was reviewed by Children's Mercy Hospital. I've read your doctor's report on the case. Your doctor made a guess about the potential cause of the injury that was wrong. I want to speak with someone about this."

Monica replied, "Without a release signed by the child's parent, we can't release any information to you. We don't have an obligation to respond to you without a subpoena."

Her use of the word "obligation" rubbed me the wrong way. I calmly explained, "A doctor at your hospital guessed wrong, and a preverbal child was left at her residence where the abuse occurred with no ability to defend herself. I'm not trying to get anybody fired, and I don't need any information from you. I'm trying to tell you what happened so you can prevent it from happening to other people. You have an obligation to listen to me."

To pacify me, Monica said, "I'm not sure who you need to speak to on this. I'll need to research this. My supervisor is on spring break, so it might take me some time to get back to you."

I waited for Monica to call me back. When we were approaching a month, I called again because it was clear I was being ignored.

On April 15, 2019, I called risk management and spoke with a woman named Janet. I gave my name and asked for Monica.

Janet put me on hold. When she came back she said, "Monica recognized your name but unfortunately she just left for a meeting. We've passed your information on to leadership and our division is no longer involved. I'll tell leadership you called."

Instantly annoyed by being put off, I said, "Your leadership is not going to call me back. They are just hoping I stop calling. What is the name of the person in leadership that my information was passed on to?"

Janet said, "I don't know the name of the person."

"Is the name of the division that my information was passed to actually called 'leadership'? I want to speak with them directly and I want to know how to find them."

"There are lots of different leadership roles. We will find out who it is and give them a nudge."

The content of these statements was annoying, but her tone really did it for me. It was that hyper-correct, patronizing way of speaking used for people you are humoring but have no intention of helping. I was so mad that my voice was shaking when I said, "I called your hospital to tell you that one of your doctors acted poorly on a case and put a child at risk. I'm trying to *give you* information to prevent this from happening again and nobody will call me back. You're an agency that protects children, and you won't listen. If you're me, how does that look?"

Janet said, "I'm guessing not good."

I snapped, "It looks terrible. Tell *that* to leadership."

I asked for Janet's last name, which she gave, and then I ended the phone call.

I never received a follow up phone call from leadership—or anybody else—at Children's Mercy Hospital.

⌁

I attempted to contact the governor's office to alert her to how the various agencies in her state had behaved. The DCF Facebook page had quoted the governor as saying, "From day one of my administration, I've made it clear that the safety and well-being of children in Kansas is my top priority," and so I thought my information would interest her. I hit the generic *Contact Us* button on the governor's website, and right above the generated form it said, "Our office is ready to assist the people of Kansas with any questions, concerns or ideas you may have about the issues facing our state. For example, we may be able to assist you if you're not satisfied with the decision made by one of the state agencies. We may be able to act as a facilitator on your behalf." I wrote a lengthy email including a brief summary of my concerns in the text box—including that the Kansas attorney general's office didn't respond to me, Daniel Holland lied, and a child was returned to her residence where the injury occurred—and stated that I wasn't interested in getting anybody fired.

I never received any contact from the governor's office.

⌁

On July 9, 2019, Mike and I met with DCF deputy secretary Brenda Hughes in her spacious office in downtown Topeka to review my cover letter. When I finished, Hughes said that I was eligible to request expungement on August 1, 2019. She said, "That's probably the most expedient means of resolving the issue."

I pointed out, "You can overturn my finding this week if you want to." The real difference between requesting an expungement and DCF overturning a finding isn't expediency. An expungement request doesn't require DCF to admit they did anything wrong, and this would make it harder to defend myself going forward when employers asked me if I had ever been on the Child Abuse Registry.

Brenda Hughes and I agreed that she would respond to my request to overturn the finding by July 19, 2019. On July 23, she sent me an email stating that she needed more time to look things over. When August 6 rolled around and I still hadn't heard from her, I emailed asking if I should go ahead and request expungement since I was now eligible for it. That's what she was waiting for anyway. I wanted my name off the Child Abuse Registry so I could go on with my life, and if requesting an expungement would get the job done, I was willing to try it even if DCF wouldn't have to acknowledge their errors. Brenda quickly replied that I should proceed with an expungement request.

I filled out the expungement request form and sent it to DCF along with my report, my DCF cover letter, and the KBI cover letter. The expungement hearing was scheduled on September 4, 2019, and occurred in a small conference room with two DCF representatives. I had very little anxiety in the days leading up to the hearing. I had already said and done everything possible to defend myself and, just like all the others, this outcome wasn't up to me. Mike came with me, as he had always done, and I answered every question. The hearing was short and uneventful.

I received my letter signed by the DCF Secretary on September 12, 2019, 2,109 days from the start of this mess. The letter was short and read,

The Expungement Review Panel reviewed the information provided by you and West Region and recommended your name be removed from the Kansas Child Abuse & Neglect Central Registry. As Secretary of DCF, I accept the recommendation and authorize the expungement to take place upon receipt of this letter by the Kansas Child Abuse & Neglect Central Registry staff.

It didn't say anything about the fact that I shouldn't have been on the Registry in the first place, or that I was only on it because of others' incompetence, or that my life had been on hold for three years because nobody had the guts to take me off of it. The paperwork made it look like I abused a child and that DCF was nice enough to let me off the Registry—but it also meant I was free. I read it, put it back in the envelope, and filed it away with my other correspondence. Immediately after that I sat down at my computer and began my application to graduate school in social welfare at the University of Kansas.

We can't say we didn't know this happened. We can't say we don't understand how the system can fail, or that those charged with protecting our most vulnerable citizens sometimes bully them into submission instead. We can't pretend that agencies who demand accountability from clients refuse to hold themselves accountable, or that the people charged with serving the unfortunates don't occasionally care more about their image and power than doing the right thing. And now that we've made it to the end of this story, I want to talk to anyone in a position to effect change in ways either big or small: Now that we know, what are we going to do about it?

Acknowledgements

"For we are God's coworkers."

1 Corinthians 3:9

I provided the labor, but the impact of this book is up to God.

Renegade Agency would not exist without Charlotte Wilson from Bookish Edits. I felt a moral obligation to tell this story but didn't know how to do it. Charlotte's expertise was like a life raft thrown in my direction. I cannot thank her enough. I cannot recommend her enough.

A big thanks to those who post content on social media about the world of writing and publishing. Your knowledge was valuable to me in so many ways.

To Mike: Thanks for riding along on my crusade even though this wasn't exactly what we had in mind.

To Ryan, Joseph and Thomas: I love you all beyond measure, and I hope this book gives you something to be proud of.